Praise For Paul Ferrini's Books

"The most important book I have read. I study it like a bible!"
Elisabeth Kubler-Ross, M.D., author of *On Death and Dying*.

"These words embody tolerance, universality, love and compassion—hallmarks of all Great Teachings. They turn our
attention inward to our own divine nature, instead of divert-
ing it outward. Paul Ferrini is a modern-day Kahlil
Gibran—poet, mystic, visionary, teller of truth." Larry
Dossey, M.D., author of *Healing Words: The Power of Prayer
and the Practice of Medicine*.

"Paul Ferrini leads us skillfully and courageously beyond
shame, blame and attachment to our wounds into the
depths of self-forgiveness. His work is a must-read for all people who are ready to take responsibility for their own
healing." John Bradshaw, author of *Family Secrets*.

"A breath of fresh air in an often musty and cluttered
domain. With sweetness, clarity, and simplicity we are
directed to the truth within. I read this book whenever my
heart directs, which is often." Pat Rodegast, author of
Emmanuel's Book I, II and III.

"Paul Ferrini's writing is authentic, delightful and wise. It
reconnects the reader to the Spirit Within, to that place
where even our deepest wounds can be healed." Joan
Borysenko, Ph.D., author of *Guilt is the Teacher, Love is the
Answer*.

"I feel that this work comes from a continuous friendship
with the deepest part of the Self. I trust its wisdom."
Coleman Barks, poet and translator.

"Paul Ferrini's wonderful books show a way to walk lightly
with joy on planet earth." Gerald Jampolsky, M.D., author of
Love is Letting Go of Fear.

"Paul Ferrini leads us on a gentle journey to our true source
of joy and happiness—inside ourselves." Ken Keyes, Jr.,
author of *The Handbook of Higher Consciousness*.

Book Design by Paul Ferrini
Typesetting by Nancy Jean Barmashi

All Artwork by Lucy Mueller White

For my son, Misha

ISBN # 1-879159-17-1

Manufactured in the United States of America

WAKING UP TOGETHER

Illuminations
on the Road to Nowhere

PAUL FERRINI

TABLE OF CONTENTS

PREFACE: THE ROAD TO NOW HERE 9

PART ONE: A ROAD WITHOUT
           A DESTINATION

Entrance 17

Truth and Paradox 30

A Change of Heart 33

The Whole Elephant 38

PART TWO: HONORING SELF & OTHER

A Few Simple Truths 45

What Can Be Shared 51

Partnership 52

Ecstasy 56

A Safe Space 58

Two Gifts of Spirit 59

PART THREE: MOVING INWARD

The Journey to Peace .63

Peeling Away 68

Beginnings and Endings .70

What is Not 75

The Invisible Car 79

Part Four: An Open Reed

To Think or Not to Think 85

Self-Discovery 88

Authenticity 94

One Self 97

Part Five: The Lessons Of Relationship

The Betrayal of Self 103

Pushing Through 105

Self-Nurturing 107

Love is Not Need 111

Seeking is Not Finding .114

The Divine Dance 117

Part Six: Knowing and Not Knowing

Not Knowing 123

Not Deciding for Others 126

Dismantling the Authority of the Ego 129

Observing the Observer .136

Part Seven: Tao/Grace

Accepting Life as it is .145

Resting in the Heart .146

The Manifestation Process 148

Willingness Vs. Willfulness 153

The Empty Vessel 157

Part Eight: Commandments & Uncommandments

Hearing our Inner Voice 165

The Peace Process 166

Commandments 172

The Golden Rule 176

The Power of Humility 180

Part Nine: Being Where We Are

Romance and Despair .187

Mirror, Mirror, on the Wall 192

Facing the Music 197

Awareness of Separation 199

Surrendering our Concepts of Perfection 202

Forgiveness Meditation 205

Moving Beyond Ego 207

A Final Blessing 212

THE ROAD TO NOW HERE

Nowhere is not a bad place. It's just the place you come to when you stop avoiding this moment, when you stop trying to find a better place than the place where you are. When you look closely at the word Nowhere, you notice that it is composed of two words: NOW and HERE. When we finally realize that all of the roads to somewhere lead to this place and this moment, our proposed destination doesn't matter much any more. "Where are you going?" our companion asks. "Oh, Nowhere in particular," we answer, content to be where we are and knowing that we oftentimes don't end up where we think we are going. "I'm just traveling this road because it stretches out before me...I'm not really sure where it leads."

Willie Nelson and Jack Kerouac aren't the only ones "on the road again." We're all on the road. Life is perpetual motion. Even if we endeavor to stay in one place, change will find us and push us out the door.

We are all on the road. Some of us actually think we

know where we are going. But sooner or later, we'll find out that was just a strange conceit.

You can plan your journey as much as you like. You can take suitcases full of clothes, even some of your favorite furniture if you want, but it will all be for naught. In the end, you will have to give up all the baggage of your past and every idea you have of the future. You see, you can't prepare for this moment. You can't anticipate this place. It just can't be done.

You can try to do it, but you will be disappointed. You can keep trying and keep getting distraught when your pictures of the future don't match reality as it unfolds. That's the promise and the disappointment you'll find as long as you think you are going somewhere.

But there will come a time when you know without a doubt that you aren't going where you think you are going. There will come a time when someone asks you where you are going and you'll say "I have no idea." And you won't even feel anxious when the words come out of your mouth.

Once you know you aren't going anywhere in particular, you begin to relax, because you realize that there's no rush. You don't have to "break your neck" getting some place on schedule.

As you may expect, there are no accidents on the *Road to Nowhere.* Sure, people occasionally bump into one another, but no harm is done and there are no hard feelings. People can't help being where they are, and sometimes more than one person occupies the same space and time. There's nothing to be done about it.

You have as many companions as you need on the *Road to Nowhere.* But after you've been on the road for a while, you realize that the journey doesn't have a lot to do with anyone else. It's primarily about you.

You are the subject. No, not metaphysics or healing or anything else outside yourself. You are the subject: your thoughts, your feelings, your words, and your actions. If you are willing to turn your attention to these, then you will enter the path fully.

When you leave the *Road to Somewhere,* you stop

losing yourself in the world; you turn within. *The Road to Nowhere* is the path to your own heart. It leads through all your fears and self-deceptions to reveal the shining truth about yourself.

Not many people want to know the truth about themselves or about others. That's okay. There are plenty of imaginary roads to travel that skirt the truth or keep it at a safe distance. But after a while, those roads do not satisfy. You've been in all the stores. You've played miniature golf for the four hundredth time. There's nothing to do that you haven't already done, except admit that you are going nowhere.

That admission will change your life. There's certainly no doubt that it brought you to this book. Welcome to the place you never left, though you have journeyed far and wide. Welcome to time that does not change, although the sun still rises and sets and the moon still waxes and wanes, pulling and pushing the tides.

A single moment of honesty can change a life, bringing it full circle. Nothing is different on the *Road to Nowhere* than it is on the *Road to Somewhere,* except your awareness. But that makes all the difference.

PART ONE

A ROAD WITHOUT
A DESTINATION

I am large.
I contain multitudes.
–Walt Whitman

ENTRANCE

Some time ago I wrote this little poem, or to put it more accurately, it just popped into my mind:

There is no net,

only the open sky

holding our tears.

There is no animal,

only the pain

unraveling.

There is no God,

only us

stepping into

our Divinity.

It is not easy to watch our idols fall. Our parents were not perfect, yet they deserve our love all the same. Our teachers were not perfect either, nor were our friends and lovers. Those who cared about us, though they wounded us or betrayed us in reaction to their own pain, did the best they could.

There is no one to blame. Those we have condemned have learned to put the past behind them, or they soon will. They have gone on with their lives and so must we.

There is no one to praise. Those we have lifted up onto some pedestal have fallen into the mud and mire of existence. The Gurus have all been caught with their hands in the candy jar.

There are no men or women better than we are. Nor are there any who are worse. No one to look up to. No one to look down upon.

There is no teaching better than any other. Every intellectual system — scientific, theological, esoteric, metaphysical — comes to a reality it can neither describe or account for. Every holy scripture has been distorted in translation and obviated by the words and actions of believers who profess to uphold it.

There is no net to hold our tears. We are disenchanted, disabused. Our balloons have been deflated. Our fantasies have hit the ground and broken into tiny pieces. Human beings have let us down. Ideas have betrayed us.

We have learned the hard way that there is no one outside our own experience to praise or to blame for our condition. Where we are, we have arrived by our-selves. True, certain people have contributed to our direction, but not a single one of those people is responsible for it. We bear that responsibility ourselves.

We sit alone with our pain and our joy. The embell-ishment on either end is gone. The highs and the lows have been demystified. At last, we have contacted the ground of our being.

And where is God in this strange equation of our aloneness? For many, God is the answer to our power-lessness, the final authority in an emotional landscape crying out for boundaries. We may not know what is going on, but God does. Our faith in Him is like a pill or a panacea, an addiction to hope that temporarily takes the pain away.

Faith like this may last for a while, but in the end it self-destructs. When we stand like Job in the midst of our suffering, the God of absolutes has no answers for us. Only God within has words for us, the still, small voice that addresses us not just on the mountaintop, but in the valleys of our experience, the one who brings love in the midst of our aloneness, our pain, our disconnection.

When we meet the divine within our own hearts and experience, we know that our spiritual journey is not a linear one. It moves up and down and all around. And wherever we are is where we must learn to be present fully. Wherever we find ourselves is where our spirituality must be.

In the old days we went to the church, the temple, or the ashram looking for God. And we found all manner of authority figures who promised us salvation. We learned their theologies, studied their scriptures, investigated their esoterica only to come up disillusioned, disgruntled, overwhelmed by the emotional demands of our everyday life which refused to be placated by words or concepts.

Now we know the outcome of that external search. The authority we seek cannot be found outside ourselves. If we want authentic spirituality, we must find it at home. We must find it in the warp and woof of our daily existence.

Welcome to the *Road to Nowhere*, the only road that does not promise you a destination. After following the *Road to Somewhere* through endless detours, this unpretentious road is a welcome sight. "No praise. No Blame," the sign says. "Enter only if you are ready to be where you are."

Contrary to popular opinion, the *Road to Nowhere* is a real road. It is just like the *Road to Somewhere*, except that it has no particular destination. Or if it does have a destination, you don't know what it is, so it might as well not have one. Indeed, knowing where the road goes would not help you. On the *Road to Nowhere* you have a distinct advantage not knowing where you are going.

The *Road to Nowhere* stands directly before you. And you will set out upon it, for no other reason than it is there and so are you. You will walk it backwards and forwards. You will stray from the path and return to it many times. You will have lots of thoughts about what it all means and where you are going. But they will simply be mental chatter. They won't mean anything. None of your thoughts will deliver you from the road or make it end sooner.

Those of you who have walked the road less traveled never knew it would come to this. You thought you'd find the same God encountered by the pilgrims. But not so. That God is dead. That God has abdicated. He no longer wants the responsibility for your life.

Welcome to road where God is everywhere and nowhere at the same time. Welcome to the place where knowing is based on realizing that you know nothing.

There is a road going by but you don't know where it is going. Standing by the side of the road, you don't know whether to go right or left, or whether to stay where you are. You don't know.

Sooner or later, out of boredom no doubt, you will

make a choice. You will go right or left. And you will get excited thinking that you have made the right decision until you come to difficult terrain, and then you will be convinced that you went the wrong way. This will happen whether you go right or left. It makes no difference.

Sometimes it will seem that the experiences that occur in your life are the result of the choices that you have made. Other times, it will be clear to you that these experiences would have occurred regardless of what you chose and when you chose it.

Every attempt you make to figure out the meaning of your life will be frustrated. That is the nature of the *Road to Nowhere*. Everybody is on it. But only a few people know they are on it. Only a few have given up trying to figure their lives out. Only a few have surrendered, walking the road for the sake of walking, taking each experience as it comes, without judging it as good or bad, without analyzing it or interpreting it. Only a few people walk the road, breathing deeply, eyes alert to everything around them, content to go wherever the path leads.

A Road Without A Destination

Every person journeys on the *Road to Nowhere*, but most people are convinced they are going somewhere. Until the car breaks down or they fall down a ravine! Then they know they weren't going where they thought they were going. But even the majority of those people get up, dust themselves off, and buy a ticket to a different destination. They stay on the road, thinking they are going to a different place than the one they went to before.

They do not know that there are no different places. All places are the same on the *Road to Nowhere*. All experiences lead to the same place. And that place cannot be described.

You have heard of the *Cloud of Unknowing*. Perhaps that makes more sense to you. Clouds are blown about by the wind. They aren't going anywhere in particular. You can relate to a cloud going nowhere, but you can't relate to a road going nowhere. Why is this?

Perhaps because you built the road. You know where it leads, or you think you do.

You didn't know it would come to this, did you? No praise. No blame. No intellectual solutions. No one to fix, not even yourself. Nothing in particular to say or to do.

Or perhaps you knew and didn't want to face it. So you went to work on the 22nd floor, or you got married and had kids. Or you found a hobby or a meditation teacher. But none of that worked.

Now, perhaps, it doesn't seem so surprising. Nothing works on the *Road to Nowhere*, unless you don't expect it to work. Then it works.

Have you ever tried living with no expectations. It's a non-sequitor, is it not? How can you "try" having no expectations? You can't. No expectations only happens when your expectations just drop, either through total exasperation or total boredom. It just happens and you notice it. But as soon as you try to duplicate it, it stops.

God doesn't perform for anyone. God just happens too.

On the *Road to Nowhere*, all you have is God, but it isn't the God of the Old Testament or the New

Testament. It is the trickster God. The one Jesus didn't tell us about until now, and the only reason he's telling us now is that he has revealed himself as a TRICKSTER. Only a trickster can worship a peekaboo God.

You see, the God we have been worshipping for thousands of years is not available to us any more. Nor is the Jesus who died on the cross. That Jesus has come and gone. We don't need him anymore. We are all doing an excellent job carrying our own crosses. We don't need Jesus to die for our sins anymore. We're doing just fine dying for our own sins.

When Jesus speaks to us now, the basic message is the same, but the reference points, the symbols, are totally different. The gospel on the *Road to Nowhere* is not the same gospel that called Peter, Luke or John.

They needed a road with a destination, a different one perhaps than the one others were taking, but a road to a destination all the same. They too were on the *Road to Nowhere*, but they didn't know it. And Jesus couldn't tell them, because they wouldn't have answered the call if he told them that the goal itself was an illusion.

Very few will answer the call now. Not many people want to know that they are already enlightened. That teaching doesn't sell much product. It drives the software and hardware people crazy. It's anti-consumer. There's nothing to buy, because nothing is missing.

When Jesus came before, he was a good salesman. This time, he's not trying to sell anything. How can a trickster sell a peekaboo God? Who wants to buy it?

Finally, a teaching that can't be bought or sold! Yet that doesn't mean people won't try to do it. You yourself probably bought this book. You might even be inspired to give workshops on it. But you will be wasting your time, just as you are wasting your time reading this book. There is nothing in this book that you don't already know and that everybody else doesn't already know.

The best this book can do is remind you of what you know in your gut to be true but have forgotten or ignored, perhaps because you didn't want to face the naked truth. But facing that truth really isn't so painful. And all the time you spent on the *Road to Somewhere* was not wasted. After all, it got you to the *Road to Nowhere*. And even though you were on that road all the time, you didn't know that you were. So there has been progress, so to speak.

Anyway, welcome home.

Here you won't find any recipes for enlightenment, because you are already enlightened. You just don't want to admit it to yourself or anyone else.

It's time to come out of the closet. Admit that the truth is in you and has always been. Celebrate the smashing of idols, the crashing of belief systems, gurus and all forms of external authority. Celebrate that fact the truth for you is known within. Celebrate the fact that you don't have to give this truth to anyone else because they already have it. No more priests, missionaries, rabbis, buddhas or bodhisatvas. No more teachers or preachers, leaders or followers. What you have belongs to all. It's like air. It's in universal circulation. It would be preposterous to try to buy or sell it.

Most of what we value is what we think is lacking in

us. It is not missing, but we think it is. And every "filler" is a substitute, a sham. We spend our lives chasing what we cannot find and do not really need. A puzzling fact, don't you think?

Yes, it is time to come out. It is time to shout it to the rafters. Nobody has what I need, because what I need is an illusion. There's no cure, because there is no disease. There's nobody in here or out there who needs to be fixed.

Yahoo! It's the truth. And it has made us free to travel the *Road to Nowhere* unabashed. Indeed, it's our favorite hike. Every time we do this trail, something new and interesting happens. This hike is only boring/exciting or pleasant/distressing if we compare it to the last.

On the *Road to Nowhere*, there is no time. No past, no future. And therefore only a timeless present impossible to delineate or describe. To talk about the road you must walk it. And the more you walk it, the less talk seems necessary.

Truth and Paradox

Truth is paradoxical. To grasp the whole of it, you must approach it from both sides. One sided approaches lead only to half-truths.

The world of perception is composed of half-truths. It is as untrue as it is true, as distorted as it is clear.

The statement "God is within" may seem to be a simple truth. Yet it is easily misunderstood. What is it that God is within? The mind? The heart? Our experience?

If God is in the mind, is God in my attack thoughts? If God is in the heart, is it in my anger? If God is in my experience, is it in the way I perceive my life?

"Perhaps," you may concede. But isn't the opposite also true? Is it not also just as true that God is not in my thoughts, my emotions, and my perceptions of my life, because all these are limited?

Only when you say God is within and without do you begin to approach truth. God is within my experience, yet it is also outside and beyond my experience.

When I say "This is it," I must also concede "This isn't really it at all." Both are true simultaneously. Or to say it another way, both are equally untrue.

You cannot make any statement to the exclusion of its opposite and approach truth. All statements that do not concede the equal truth of their opposites are simply opinion. They are subjective, self-indulgent perceptions of reality.

Until we concede the paradoxical nature of reality, we will never transcend conflict in thoughts or action, consciousness or relationship. For everything you think is true, there is something else equally true that contradicts it.

As soon as you concede the validity of the opposite point of view, you move out of duality. A perfect example of this is the concept of "Detente" which, as it became accepted in the greater consciousness, led to the dismantling of the Berlin wall and the ending of the Cold War.

Transcendence of conflict comes from mutual respect. Mutual respect comes from regard for the opinions of others.

All opinion is equally important or unimportant. Black is as good as White.

If you insist on agreement or synthesis, if you say "black and white must become grey" in order for duality and conflict to be transcended, you will wait a long time. But if you say, "black is fine as black; white is fine as white. Both are equally acceptable," then black and white cease to be in opposition. When there is mutual acceptance of both positions, the basis of conflict is literally dissolved.

It is ironic. We spend our whole lives looking for agreement, thinking it will make us happy, but the very search for agreement creates the conditions for our unhappiness.

The search for agreement is simply the search to be right, to have one's opinions reinforced by others. The more we seek agreement the more we find disagreement. Hitler, for example, received a great deal of reinforcement for his ideas. He also found a great deal of opposition.

It is the same for you and me. If we look for agreement, we will find it, but we will also find an equal amount of disagreement.

A CHANGE OF HEART

To live a life that is conflict-free is possible, but only if conflict is totally acceptable. As soon as you insist on a quiet ocean, the typhoon is born.

Accepting the polarities brings us into the heart where all things are acceptable as they are. Can we accept, for example, that we want something and do not want it at the same time? Or will we push for a decision for or against, pro or con?

To push for a decision in the face of conflict or ambivalence is a way of punishing ourselves and others. Instead, let us embrace both extremes of our thinking and feeling. Let us acknowledge all the things we want about the job or the relationship and all of the things that make us want to run away. Then we will have our arms around all of it.

Let us embrace the totality of our experience and live with its inherent contradictions, knowing that choice is impossible until our inner dynamic shifts. Being with conflict and ambivalence brings a peaceful acceptance from which clarity springs.

If you try to deal with ambivalence at the mental level you will only deepen it. But if you bring it all into the heart, into the depths of your being where you are vast, where you contain multitudes of contradictory propositions in an embrace of patience and compassion, then ambivalence loses its edge and its urgency.

Conflict held in a loving manner does not threaten to split us apart in our thoughts or in our interactions with each other. Ambivalence held with the blessing of self-love and compassion for others does not lead to separation.

How do you do this? How do you hold the contradictions of your mental/emotional states in a loving embrace?

You begin by seeing the urgency in yourself. You see how desperate you are to choose and how this pressure to choose is a way of pushing the conflict away.

And instead you welcome the conflict. You say, "I welcome the parts of me which are at war with each other. I am the peacemaker. I accept you as you are. I respect your opinions. I will not act in a way that violates you.

I am the peacemaker. I am large enough to contain these contradictions, to hold them patiently and silently. I do not have to choose now and so dishonor a part of myself. I will honor all of me, however long it takes.

I am the peacemaker. I am the one who brings all conflict and ambivalence into the heart's quiet embrace. I am the one who brings a safe space for conflict to be."

When there is safety, conflict can be encompassed. Where there is safety, all of the split parts of myself can be honored and heard.

Lest I learn to do this within my own consciousness, how can I do it in my relationship with you? If I cannot give safety to myself how can I give it to you?

What does it mean to still the mind? It means to accept its contents with loving attention. All of its contents. Inclusively. All the judgments, doubts, the fears, the incriminations. To accept each as it arises, not because it is right or wrong, but because it is there. To accept what is, without interpretation. To be present for self. To bring all the parts of self together in one patient moment of attention. What is a still mind, but a compassionate one? Not a mind free of conflict, but a mind in which conflict is patiently accepted.

As long as we are trying to get rid of conflict, we deepen it. As long as we are trying to choose between different points of view, we are sharpening the edge that divides them. The pressure to decide when we are in conflict is a two-edged sword. It appears to offer relief, but in reality it exacerbates the wound.

If we want to decide, we need to create a safe space to decide in. We need to step away from the pressure, the urgency. That way, we take the sword of division and love it. In our love, its edge softens. Steel fades to a simple line drawn in the sand. When the tide comes in, it takes it. There is no more division.

What does it mean to turn the sword into a plow-share? It means to end conflict in oneself by accepting the extremes of one's mental/emotional experience. It means to give loving attention to both sides, to nurture the split-off parts of one's person-hood equally, to be the parent of one's own wayward inner children, who are at odds with each other like jealous siblings.

What does it mean to be the peacemaker, but to bring peace in the face of conflict? To bring a safe space, a loving attitude. To learn to bless oneself when fear comes up.

Ego mind cannot do this. For ego-mind is at war with itself. It is divided. Only that which is not divided can bring peace.

Only the heart can speak of love when the eyes are frozen in fear. Only the heart can make the safe space for the wounded children in our lives. Only the heart can hear the screams of the ego as a call for love.

Find your heart. Find the place of safety in yourself. The place of blessing. The place of acceptance which is deeper than your fear. Find the place in which conflict can float as an overturned boat floats on the surface of the water. Find the deep ocean of compassion within. The buoyant Self in which your split off personae cohere. Find the heart. And bring the ego-mind to it.

That is where sword becomes ploughshare, where peace is born on earth. Through your surrender, your compassion. That is the blessing love gives to the soul's impatient wound.

THE WHOLE ELEPHANT

Inside every judgment I make about you is a judgment about myself. And both are equally true or false.

As long as I think I have the truth and you don't, I

create separation, inequality and the basis for suffering in my life. The same thing happens if I think you have the truth and I don't.

The reality is we both have a piece of the truth and a piece of the illusion. We look at the same elephant, but you see the tail and I see the trunk. When seen separately, tail and trunk seem to have nothing in common. Only when the whole elephant is seen do tail and trunk make sense together.

No matter how hard I try, I cannot see the meaning of your piece. Tail does not understand the why or wherefore of trunk. The only way I can come to terms with your experience is to accept it as true in the same way as I accept my experience as true. I must give your perceptions the same credibility I give my own. Until this equality is established between us, the seeds of conflict will remain.

I don't have to make you right and myself wrong. I don't have to replace my truth with yours or live my life on your terms. Nor do I have to make you wrong and insist that you live your life on my terms.

Such requests come from insecurity and the false belief that in order to love each other we must agree. That is not true. To love you, I must accept you as you are. That is all that is required.

But that is a lot! Accepting you as you are is as profound a proposition as accepting myself as I am. It is a formidable task, because I have so little experience at it.

Letting you have your experience is the beginning. I learn to honor what you think and feel, even when I don't like it or agree with it. Even when it upsets me.

Rather than make you responsible for the pain I feel in relation to you, I learn to look at my own pain. My reaction to your experience – positive or negative – gives me information about myself. My commitment to myself and to you is to work with my own pain, not to make you responsible for it.

Only when I can give you back the gift of your own experience, without imposing my own thoughts and feelings on it, do I love you without conditions. By accepting your experience as it is, by not needing to change it, I honor you as a spiritual being.

My thoughts and feelings matter in and of themselves, not as a commentary on or indictment of your experience. By communicating how I think or feel, without making you responsible for my thoughts and feelings, I am able to have my experience and let you have your experience too.

In relationships, as in consciousness, both sides of the coin must be accepted as equal. One cannot move out of conflict with another until the experience of both people has been honored.

Agreement is never the issue, although it seems to be. The issue is always: can we honor each other's experience?

When we feel that the other person accepts us as we are, we have the motivation to accommodate each other. To accommodate is to make room for the other next to us, not to impose or be imposed on.

Once accommodation happens, the two of us dwell together. Man with woman. Black with white. Rich with poor. Jew with Gentile. To accept our differences is to honor our common humanity, to bless each other at the deepest level of our shared experience.

So trunk and tail can argue until they are blue in the face and neither will win the argument. Both experiences are equally valid. By allowing them, the elephant begins to take shape.

By accepting the validity of your experience, without trying to change it, without trying to make it look more like mine, the greater meaning of my own experience begins to emerge. When I see you as an equal partner, not as someone who needs to be educated, reformed or fixed, the significance of our relationship reveals itself. As each part is welcomed, the whole begins to take shape and the significance of the parts is better understood and appreciated.

A world that is looking for agreement will find factionalism and conflict. A world that makes a safe space for diversity will find the core unity that makes it whole.

Opposites can be resisted or embraced. Resisted, they externalize as conflict between self and other. Accepted, they integrate as dynamic agents creating the alchemical transformation within the Self.

PART TWO

HONORING SELF

AND OTHER

A Few Simple Truths

Reading a lot of words is exhausting. We do not need a lot of words. The more words we have, the more we argue about what they mean. And the more we argue, the less we understand.

There are only two things you or anyone else needs to understand. First, you need to understand that your experience is perfect for you. In spite of what you may think or others may think, there is nothing about you or your experience that needs to be changed or fixed.

On the other hand, your experience is your teacher. You are in constant dialogue with it. If you are willing, you can learn a great deal from it. This is true whether or not you like your experience. In fact, most of what you will learn in this lifetime has to do with coming to grips with the aspects of your experience you have trouble accepting. That is where your growth is.

The other thing you need to understand is that the experience of other people is perfect the way it is. Like you, they do not need to be reformed, educated or fixed. They are encountering the lessons they need to grow and become more loving, accepting human beings.

If you know these two facts, and practice your awareness of them, you will create less suffering in your life.

One way to practice your awareness is to stop judging, blaming or crucifying yourself. If you can't do that, then just be aware of your self-judgments and work on forgiving them, undoing them, recognizing that they do not tell the truth about you.

Another way to practice this awareness is to stop judging, blaming, crucifying other people. When judgments come up about other people, realize that these judgments say very little about anyone else. They do indicate parts of your own heart-mind that are crying out for acceptance and healing. Become aware of the times when you find fault with others and let them off the hook. Then you can take the hook out of your own mouth.

These are two simple practices. I offer them to you as tools that will transform your life. The words and concepts are simple. The challenge lies in the practice.

You can spend your whole life chasing complicated solutions to your problems, but it will be a waste of time. The answers are simple. And they are close at hand.

To find them, begin to look inside. Nobody else has the answer for you. Nor do you have the answer for anyone else.

Nobody else can make you happy. Nobody else can make you sad. Your happiness or sadness belongs only to you.

Do not look to someone to save you from your sins. It will not happen. All self-professed saviors are wolves in sheep's clothing.

Nor blame someone else for your mistakes. Nobody else can be made responsible for what you believe or the choices you make.

Keep these simple truths in front of you at all times and act accordingly. The way is straight. It appears to be crooked only when you try to twist it to meet your own mis-perceived needs.

Be clear about these boundaries. All trespass happens because of lack of clarity about what responsibility belongs to you and what responsibility belongs to others.

You are responsible for you. Others are responsible for themselves.

Do what you can do for yourself. Do not ask someone else to do for you what you can and should do for yourself. Do not give your power away.

Do what you can do for others. Give help when it is asked for and you can give it freely. But do not take on more than you can do with a willing heart.

It is important to help others when you can, but do not do for them what they must learn to do for themselves. If you insist on taking false responsibility for others, you invite their blame when what you do is not to their liking.

You were not elected as a savior. So please don't try to be one.

Let me give you this hint: all saviors will be crucified. All who are placed on a pedestal will be tarred and feathered and driven through the muck. Please consider this before you climb the podium and tell people you have the answers for them.

Everyone who is raised up by men and women will be stoned by them at some other time. That is the nature of projection.

It all comes from bad boundaries, from not knowing what your responsibility is and isn't.

Nobody but you is responsible for your pleasure or your pain. Not your lover. Not your enemy.

And even you may not be responsible at a conscious level. So do not crucify yourself if you are in pain. Just let the pain be your teacher.

The role of others in your life is not to do for you or to tell you what to do, but to support you in discovering the truth about yourself. And that is also your role in their lives.

Your role is to be a friend to others, and to be open to the friendship they offer you. You do not have to carry them, nor do they have to carry you. Only children need to be carried, and not for as long as you might think.

Even if you can do the task better than your brother

can, you must let him do it. Whatever he has chosen belongs to him. Stand back and make room for him. Don't even look over his shoulder.

When someone – adult or child – wants to learn from you, be a role model. Demonstrate what needs to be done by doing it. Let them watch you and practice what you do. When they have learned what you can teach them, send them on their way.

Do not foster dependency in others. When you have offered help and it has been received, celebrate that moment and set the person free.

When the student keeps coming back for more instruction, you know a dependent pattern is there. Do not encourage it, even if it benefits you financially.

Believe in others even when they do not believe in themselves. Tell them you know that they can do it and set them free.

A good teacher empowers the student. A good therapist helps her client learn the skills she needs to make it on her own.

We are here to facilitate the progress of others, not

to hold onto them. And we can only teach what we ourselves are willing to learn.

What Can Be Shared

All relationships offer fulfillment, but most do not deliver it, because people become co-dependent. They take false responsibility for others and not enough responsibility for self. And then they blame others for their misfortunes. It is a vicious cycle.

One can be happy with another. One can be sad with another. Joy and sadness can be shared. But one's joy is not the other's responsibility, nor is one's sadness. All thoughts and feelings are our own responsibility.

Until we know that, it is almost impossible to live successfully with another person. Even when we do know it, remembering it in our partner's presence becomes a constant spiritual practice.

To "be with" another is an ecstatic experience, just as it is ecstatic to "be with" ourselves. But "being with" is a moment to moment act. It has nothing to do with what our ego wants or what our partner's ego wants.

My ego wants you to "be there" for me whether you want to or not. My ego wants to blame you for my unhappiness. My ego wants you to do things the way I want them done. And no matter what you try to do to satisfy my ego, it will never be satisfied, because it won't take responsibility for its own happiness.

As soon as ego takes responsibility, it ceases to be ego. And then I stop demanding things from you. I begin to accept you as you are. I surrender to the present moment, to the truth of who I am and you are. That is the moment of true joining, when the boundaries between us fade, not because they are inappropriate, but because they have been totally honored. That is the moment when two become one, without losing what they are, without sacrifice, without expectation. That is a moment of total bliss, a moment when the promise of love without conditions is fulfilled.

PARTNERSHIP

I don't know why anyone would think that loving another person would be any easier than loving oneself.

If you have trouble being kind to yourself, accepting your mistakes with compassion, forgiving your judgments, walking through your fears, how can you expect to do the same for another? If you have trouble bringing love to the wounded child within who is crying out in pain, how can you bring love to wounded aspects of your partner's being?

It is not possible to offer your partner what you are unable to offer yourself. To attempt to do so will only bring pain to yourself and the other.

You need to start where you are, not where you wish you were. If you are angry, you must start with your anger. If you are lonely, insecure, seeking validation through others, you must bring your awareness there.

I don't say that you can't do this in a relationship. You certainly can, if both people have the willingness to help each other look at their wounds.

But to help your partner look at her wounds requires that you accept her just as she is. If you need to change her, fix her, analyze her, you cannot create a safe space for her to look at her pain.

She can look at her pain only when she feels safe being with it. And she can feel safe only when she knows she is not being judged.

Love is built on acceptance and trust, not on judgment and interpretation.

Creating a safe space is an easy thing to do when you can leave your fears behind. You have all done this for other people at some time in your life. You have risen to the occasion of their need and set your own issues aside. You have been there for them, perhaps not with words, but with your presence, your caring, your emotional support.

I am not talking about something you don't know how to do.

But it isn't easy to create a safe space for others when your own buttons are being pushed, when your own fear is rising, when your mind is going crazy with one judgment after another. It isn't even easy to create a safe space for yourself. Yet that is what you must learn to do.

You must learn to be in fear without beating yourself up, without projecting your self-judgment onto others. You must learn to make fear your companion and to walk with it. You must know what your fear is about and what your pain is about before you try to step beyond them.

When you have walked patiently with pain and fear, you are led to a deeper place of compassion with yourself. You are led into the heart. And in the heart, you feel not only your own pain and fear, but the pain and fear of everyone you meet.

To love is to be in the heart. You cannot love from any other place.

Love is not a magic potion. It is not the raging of hormones. It has very little to do with sexuality, although sexuality can be an expression of love.

Love is the acceptance of your partner as she is. It is about letting her into your heart.

There are no techniques that can take you there. There is just your own love and acceptance of yourself. That alone calls to the beloved and tells her she is welcome.

Every time you are able to feel another person's pain without feeling responsible for it, without trying to change it or fix it, just feeling it in your heart, you rest in arms of love.

There is nothing complex or esoteric here. But there is a great challenge and endless opportunities to practice.

ECSTASY

To love yourself is an ecstatic act. But loving yourself requires practice from moment to moment. It means learning to embrace your pain with your pleasure, your sadness with your joy, your failures with your successes. It means learning to trust your guidance and accepting your mistakes as opportunities to learn, grow and be more in-tune with yourself and others. The more you love yourself moment to moment, the more the spiritual adult learns to embrace the wounded kid and the more the imperfect, mistake-prone kid learns to accept her divine perfection.

If you have touched the beloved within yourself in this way, then it will not be difficult for you to touch the beloved in your partner. You understand that, like you, she is acceptable in this moment, even when she is cranky and judgmental. You see through her persona to the real person. Just as you learn to embrace contradictory states of consciousness in yourself, you learn to embrace your partner's contradictions, her awkwardness and unfinishedness.

In embracing what is, all that you thought was lacking is found to be present. Your beloved is the perfect beloved for you. Indeed, each moment as it unfolds is the perfect moment, if you can accept it unconditionally.

Perfection is never found in the outside object. It is found in the attitude of the one who looks. When the lens through which you look is clear, all objects seen through that lens are beautiful.

Ecstasy does not depend on anyone else. It requires only your presence. When you are present, heaven reveals itself in all its glory. Without your presence, there is no ecstasy.

You see, it does not matter who the beloved is.

Anyone can be the beloved, if you are present. Any situation can be ecstatic when you surrender to it, when you accept it without judgment.

A SAFE SPACE

There is no way you can anticipate what will happen in your life. There is no way you can plan for it. The next moment is always a total surprise.

After all, you are on the *Road to Nowhere.* Tomorrow you could literally be anywhere. The fact that you wake up in the same bed that you woke up in yesterday is no proof that you will wake up there tomorrow.

You think it's proof, but it's not. It's just part of the pattern you are habitually extending. But all habits come to an end, because they lose energy. And without energy, you can't live. So you will find a way to liberate yourself from your own sluggish patterns.

Everyone needs energy to live. And energy depends on transformation, on growth in consciousness. When there is an expansion of consciousness, form cracks. A —new form becomes necessary.

The more you grow in consciousness, the more you move through various forms. It can be a little disorienting. It can feel a little unsafe.

That is why it is so important that you learn to create a safe space for yourself. A space of self-nurturing. And if you are in a partnership, you need to know how to create that safe space together on an ongoing basis.

To move forward in growth, there must be assimilation and grounding of the new material. New forms must be inhabited fully.

You cannot withstand the explosion of form in your life without coming to embrace yourself with great compassion. You cannot grow and change with your partner without learning to offer each other unconditional acceptance and love.

Two Gifts of Spirit

Divine Mother gives love. Divine Father gives freedom. Together they give love without conditions, or love given freely.

The nature of Mother's love is to ground and

attach. The nature of Father's love is to liberate and extend. Both are necessary. Mother brings nurturing. Father brings growth.

Every person needs both mother and father. Every partnership needs mother's love and father's love. The man must be able to nurture and sustain as well as the woman. The woman must be able to detach and grow as well as the man.

Father brings the gift. Mother accepts it and puts it to use. Without mother, father's gift would go unnoticed. Without father, mother's gift would close in on itself.

The opposites dwell within and that is where we must learn to dance. But we must also learn to dance with each other. It is really one process, not two. Inner and outer just reflect each other. My dance with me is not dissimilar from my dance with you. And my dance with you takes me deeper into my own process.

PART THREE

MOVING INWARD

THE JOURNEY TO PEACE

When you finally understand that you are on the *Road to Nowhere*, it no longer matters where in particular you are going. All locations are the same. All relationships are the same. All forms of escape are the same.

When you are firmly committed to your journey regardless of where it takes you, it ceases to be an external one. External situations are irrelevant. The real journey is the journey to peace within your own heart. And that journey is happening in the present all the time.

The only question that can be asked on the inward journey is "Am I at peace?" If I am not at peace, then I have identified with something outside of me. I have made my happiness conditional on something else.

So if I am not at peace, realizing this brings me back to peace. Peace is always there. It seems to disappear only because I turn my attention elsewhere.

Spiritual practice is about being peaceful moment to moment and bringing our awareness back to the present when our attention wanders to the past or future. It is about being in acceptance of our life as it unfolds, and not wanting it to be different. For as soon as we desire something other than what is, we create conflict. This conflict is not real in itself. It is just a reflection of our lack of acceptance.

If everything is acceptable as it is and nothing needs to be fixed or improved upon, what do I do with my life? That is a good question. When you reach that question, not as intellectual exercise, but as an emotional necessity, you will have the answer. But the answer will not come from anything you already know. It won't come from your ego, although the ego will propose many solutions. The ego may ask that question, but it cannot answer it.

The answer comes from beyond that place where ego can go. The answer comes from a place where there is no compulsion to act, where actions sponta-neously arise without deliberation or struggle, without attachment to outcome. You simply see what needs to be done and do it.

Having taken action, you are no longer defined by it. Having put out a fire, you do not become a fireman.

What you do in one moment does not define for you what you will do in the next. Each moment unfolds with its own integrity, its own requirements. Your job is just to be present, to be at peace, and to let words and actions come from that peaceful presence.

When you speak and act and you are not at peace, you can only attack or defend. Acting from agitation creates greater agitation. And so the cycle of suffering proliferates.

If you want to be free from suffering, you must stop creating suffering in your life. "But how do I do that?" you ask. You do that by asking the question "Am I at peace in this moment?" before you speak or act. And if you are not at peace, you take a deep breath and bring your awareness back to the present moment.

All suffering originates in your own mind. And that is where it is undone.

Continue your practice to include your thoughts and feelings. Whenever you think or feel something, ask "Am I at peace right now?" And if you are not at peace, take a deep breath and bring your awareness back to the present moment. Do not let your thoughts and feelings run amuck, or you will have to live your life through their filters.

Every thought, every feeling is a filter. Every word that is spoken and every action taken limits truth in some way. Truth itself neither thinks nor feels, speaks nor acts. Thus it never strays from itself. To rest in the truth, question each thought and feeling, each word and action. "Am I at peace right now?" And if you are not at peace, bring your awareness back to the present moment. When you can be in the moment free of thoughts or feelings about thoughts, free of the need to speak or act, then you will dwell in the heart of truth.

The heart of truth and your heart are the same. What separates you from the truth of your heart is your thoughts, feelings, words, and actions. What separates you are your filters, your interpretations.

Whenever you think you know what anything means, you have strayed from the heart of truth. For in the heart of truth, you do not need to know anything. You do not need to do anything. Everything that happens is acceptable exactly the way it is.

When external seeking for truth is no longer valued, when internal interpretations of experience are no longer indulged, there is nothing that stands between you and the supreme reality.

Nobody can tell you what that reality looks like. The attempt to picture it is absurd. All pictures are just filters.

Once you enter truth, the ego dies, for it can get no foothold. But the ego is not assassinated. It dies into truth. It surrenders. It is not a painful act, but an ecstatic one.

Peeling Away

The supreme Reality puts up no barriers to you. For you and It are one and the same.

All the barriers are put in place by you.

Finding truth is therefore not a getting of something you do not have. It is a peeling away of your filters, your interpretations. It is a surrendering of what you think you know. It is a taking down of the barriers you have erected.

That is why the journey cannot be an external one. The journey doesn't have to do with anyone else. It has to do only with you.

You are the subject. No, not metaphysics or healing or anything else outside yourself. You are the only subject: your thoughts, your feelings, your words, and your actions. If you are willing to turn your attention to these, then you will enter the path to peace.

At first it may not seem to be a very pleasant path. As you look within, you will see all of your judgments.

You will confront your fear, your pain, your loneliness. There won't be anything you can take to avoid your suffering or anesthetize it. No mood altering drugs to take, no work responsibilities or special relationships to lose yourself in. Instead, you will confront the intensity of all the judgment and fear that separates you from the Source.

But when you become aware of all these obstacles to your peace, you begin to dissolve them. You do this not by finding fault with them, but by accepting them and bringing love to yourself.

When you see that you are not at peace, you don't beat yourself up. You take a deep breath and allow peace to come. When you see that you are judging yourself or someone else, you just notice what you are doing. You just see that you are erecting obstacles to peace and you stop doing that. This practice is an "undoing," not a "doing."

Instead of finding the problem outside yourself, you see that you are the one causing your suffering. But you don't beat yourself up with this awareness.

You use this awareness to abandon judgment and return to the truth of who you are.

When you leave the *Road to Somewhere*, you stop losing yourself in the world. You become the world. Everything out there is brought within. And there, and there alone, is meaningful change possible.

In your heart you can end suffering. You cannot end it in any other place or for anyone else.

The *Road to Nowhere* is the path to your own heart. It leads through all your fears and self-deceptions. It is not a journey of escape. It is a journey through your pain to end the pain of separation.

BEGINNINGS & ENDINGS

Life appears to be linear. The sun rises in the morning and sets at night. Spring follows winter and summer follows spring.

But all that happens sequentially also happens in a cycle. Night not only follows day, but precedes it. Spring not only follows winter, but precedes it. In a circle, it is hard to know where the beginning and ending point are. Indeed, the question itself becomes meaningless.

Life is not a straight line from beginning to end, but a cycle in which every end is a beginning and every beginning an end. In each phase of the cycle, all other phases are contained.

Even though we know all this intellectually, its meaning hasn't sunk in. We still perceive our lives in a linear, sequential fashion. We still think that "A" leads to "B".

We think that we must do one thing before we can do another. For example, "I must learn to love myself before I can have a relationship with someone else." But the opposite is also true: "I must be in relationship with others if I am to learn to love myself."

Having a relationship with others and learning to love myself are happening simultaneously all the time. When I am in a relationship, I am learning to love myself. When I am alone, I am learning to be in relationship. All phases of a cycle are present in each phase.

So every moment contains all other moments. This moment contains all the past and all the future. This moment offers profound healing and reconciliation for all past or future wounds.

That is why the central teaching of all spiritual traditions is to claim our awareness in this moment. While this moment may be only one point on the circle, any point will do. Any point is the alpha and omega.

A special time or place is not needed. Here is as good a place as any; now is as good a time as any. There is nothing that you have to do first. There is nothing you have to do later. There is only what is happening now. That is your only responsibility.

You cannot be somewhere else in this moment of time. Here is the only place.

Once you realize that all that life asks of you is your simple presence, it becomes easier to surrender to the way things are. Any desire for things to be different is attachment to the past or fear of the future.

These attachments and fears are commonplace. We must not think we are unspiritual because we all have them.

Our job is not to make the attachment or the fear go away, but simply to acknowledge our resistance as it comes up. By noticing our resistance, we don't identify with it.

That is the key point. Noticing the fear, I am not that fear. Noting the attachment to a specific outcome, I am not the one who needs that outcome. So I don't have to indulge my desires or resist them. I just notice them and let them pass. As I hold each desire compassionately in awareness, it subsides.

Thoughts and feelings arise in consciousness and fade away. Nothing in particular makes them come. Nothing in particular makes them go. They are simply a diastole, like the rhythmic movement of the breath or the drum beat of the heart.

None of this means anything. It just is. It is the dance of being.

It is only when we give something meaning that

the rhythmic flow of life is interrupted. Our gestures of belief or unbelief are like trees falling across a stream. They cannot stop the stream from flowing. But they make the water work harder. A busy mind is like a chain saw. It cuts down a lot of trees. It makes the river dance wildly in many different directions.

The more the mind works, the harder it is for the body to be. And if the body cannot be present, this moment cannot be fully given or received.

So we come back to the breath, to the rising and falling of the life force within us. We come back to thoughts and feelings rising and falling in the heart/mind. And the question is: are we breathing as we think? Are we breathing as we feel? Often, we will see that we are barely breathing. The mind is moving too quickly for the body. We are somewhere else in a different time. We really aren't here at all.

The river is dancing wildly around us. But we are out of the flow of our lives. We are not at peace.

When we see that we are not at peace, we bring our attention back to the present moment. We start breathing again. Our body gets reconnected with our mind. We reclaim the place where we are.

WHAT IS NOT

The ego-mind is always asking ""What if?" It is always exploring the possibility that there may be a better place to be or a better scenario than the one that confronts us here and now. All this is motivated by fear.

Fearful of what is, the ego-mind endeavors to change it. It tries to replace "what is" with "what is not." Herein lies the root of our suffering.

The irony is that, while we think we know "what is," nothing is as we think it is. Something comes and we think it is not what we want. It turns out later it was exactly what we wanted, but we could not recognize it. Something else comes and we are certain it is exactly what we want. Later, we find out it was what we did not want in disguise.

I cannot experience anything as it is, because I have opinions about everything that occurs in my life. Spontaneous acceptance of my life in the moment is quite rare. I am always looking for some way to improve on my experience.

I am looking for a better job, a more loving partner, a more exciting place to live. I am looking outside to improve the present moment. Or I am looking to make it special, more important than other moments.

So be it. If I try to stop doing this, I will just create more conflict within. So stopping is not necessary. What is necessary is to watch my mind go into motion. As soon as I witness what it is doing, I leave automatic pilot.

When I enter the present moment with awareness, I see that my ambivalence toward life is reflected all around me. I have one hand on the door to the garage and the other on the door to the bedroom. When I finally have enough guts to enter the bedroom, I hear the car start and the garage door open. Is it me running away or is it you?

In truth, we are all running away. None of us wants to be here. Let's face it. The moment unfolded and we said "no thank you. I'd rather have a different moment."

We could choose to stay and wake up, but most of us won't. "Why?" you ask. Because most of us are totally terrified of being here fully. We are afraid we will not exist when we drop all our defenses against this moment. And, in a way, we are right. Dropping our resistance means dropping our preconceptions, our expectations, indeed all the fear-based peculiarities of our experience. Only then can we open to the moment fully. And who is it that is capable of opening to the moment fully?

It is not the limited one I think I am. He cannot open so deep and so wide.

The one who opens totally is no less than the Buddha or the Christ, the enlightened one. The one who is present without thought. The one who neither clings nor resists. The one who is complete in each moment, and who knows that each moment is acceptable exactly as it is.

It is not easy for me to think that what Jesus or Gautama did I might also do. Yet if I could not do it, how could they?

If you think Jesus or Gautama is special, you lose the whole impact of their teaching. Both said "it is possible to end suffering, right here and right now."

Not a very complex teaching, eh? Just "accept this moment as it unfolds. And if you find yourself resisting, become aware of your resistance."

That's all. You can teach this practice to a child. You don't have to make it complex.

Yet to practice this is to go to the core of our being, to go through all our doubts and fears. When we look uncompromisingly at our own resistance, we dissolve all that separates ourselves from this moment.

In our acceptance of this moment, is boundless bliss. That we can experience. That we can glimpse as we practice being present now.

THE INVISIBLE CAR

Not that I need another identity, but I often joke with my friends that now that I am losing all motivation to save myself, others, or the world, I'm going to be a beach bum. After all, I love walking on the beach and all I really know how to do any more is put one foot in front of the other.

What else can you do on the *Road to Nowhere* except put one foot in front of the other? Well, I suppose you could put one foot behind the the other, and that would work just as well.

I remember the time when I took some friends hiking in the Rio Grande Gorge in northern New Mexico. We started descending into the Gorge just as several storms were moving in. There was lightning and thunder all around us. By the time we reached the river, the rain had started to pour down. We found some temporary shelter there during the deluge and then continued our hike in the rain. Eventually, we came to the trail to the rim of the Gorge. Before heading up, we had some discussion about whether this was the right turn off. Ted and Stephanie went out ahead of us and, as we reached the top, reported that our car was not there. "We must have taken the wrong trail up," they said. So four of us — Tom, Stephanie, my son Misha and I —

headed out along the rim, looking for our car, while the others stayed behind.

After we had walked for a very long time, it became clear that we were lost. So we decided to split up. Tom and Stephanie continued walking forward and Misha and I began walking back. Our plan was a simple one: whoever found the car first would pick the others up.

As I was walking with Misha, I felt a deep peace and a great joy. "Isn't this great?" I asked Misha. "We have no idea where we are or where we are going, but the mountains and the rain are so beautiful. We're on the *Road to Nowhere* and all we have to do is follow this road, and we'll eventually get home. We're safe. It doesn't matter what happens. We don't have to worry." And we told some jokes and stories while we were walking in the rain. We were completely soaked and ragged, but it didn't matter. We had moved beyond tired, beyond the aches and pain from the steep climb to the canyon rim, beyond rain, beyond being lost, beyond looking for the car. We were ecstatic, content in that moment.

As we neared the place where we had left the majority of our party, we saw the car coming out on the dirt entrance road. It turned out that our friends had been wondering why we were taking so long when, all of a sudden, Ted looked up and saw the car. It had been there all along, but no one had seen it! So they got in the car and found us, and we eventually found Tom and Stephanie.

It had been one of the most ecstatic hikes we had been on. Sure, we almost got struck by lightning. We got soaked. We got lost. We walked five or six miles out of the way only to return to where we had started out. But none of this mattered. We thought we had taken a wrong turn, but that wrong turn was only in our minds. And regardless of the perceived wrong turn, we all knew we were safe. And we were all very glad to get home.

All this was a magnificent metaphor for our lives. We think we are somewhere, but we aren't where we think we are. Or maybe we are exactly where we are supposed to be, but we don't know it. But none of this means anything. Even if we're totally wrong about everything, so what? Nobody is going to get hurt.

We may be on the *Road to Nowhere*, but nowhere is not a bad place. It's just the place we end up when we stop avoiding this moment. It's the place where we are when we drop our expectations of the way it's supposed to be and our interpretations of "what is." It's the curving road and the magnificent, ever-changing view of the mountains without the commentary.

For Misha and me, it was a great moment. The kind of moment that happens when you fall into the heart, when you surrender totally to who and where you are.

PART FOUR

AN OPEN REED

To Think Or Not To Think

While some thinking is necessary for physical survival, most thinking makes life needlessly complex. Most thinking is a result of our lack of acceptance, our resistance to what is.

This kind of thinking comes from our small-self identification. It brings toil, planning, manipulation. It is always trying to change what is. It is thinking for or against, either/or. It moves in perpetual duality, slipping from one extreme to another, like a pendulum. There is no peace here, except perhaps for the observer.

But there is another kind of thinking. It is spontaneous and unfolds in the moment. It requires no forethought, no deliberation. It has no plan and is not attached to any outcome. This kind of thinking comes to a graceful end when the thought is expressed or the action performed. It does not perpetuate itself or create complexity.

Spontaneous thinking is aligned with the truth of our experience. It tells the truth courageously, but does not seek to make that truth true for anyone else. Spontaneous thinking is not reactive. It does not attempt to defend its experience against anyone else's.

This kind of thinking makes no enemies, for it neither attacks nor defends. It merely witnesses to its experience and holds the space for others to witness to their experience. This kind of thinking has no need to be right or to make others wrong. It can be right only because others are right too.

No exclusivity or specialness is claimed. Spontaneous thinking does not say "I am more important than you are" or "You are more important than I am." These thoughts belong to another consciousness and a different world.

Spontaneous thought is mind in the service of love and acceptance. Mind in itself is not the problem. Mind is open like a reed. If you blow through it, you will hear a flute singing. But that same mind in the service of fear, retribution, or greed becomes the housing for a poison dart. Now, when you blow, someone dies.

No, mind is not the problem. It is how mind is used.

When the reed is empty, blowing though it makes a beautiful sound, a sound that returns effortlessly to silence. When mind is still, thoughts arise spontaneously, offer themselves, and die in the wind. There is no complexity here.

The goal is not to make thinking go away, but to slow it down. To de-energize and diffuse the analytical mind so that it comes to rest in its natural container. All that stands out about the individual, all that separates and divides, rests in that which has never known division. Call it love, compassion, heart-mind. Names do not matter.

When you see which of your thoughts are restless and which are driven by fear, you no longer need to react to those thoughts. You don't have to believe them or disbelieve them. You just let them be. You just take a deep breath and watch the pendulum swing back and forth until you find your center. And then you rest in that stillness, in that peace.

Once you are there, you no longer desire to be anywhere else. Once you are there, you cannot be attacked by your thoughts or anyone else's.

Self-Discovery

The discovery of Self is not a process of finding what is true, but of peeling away what is false. What is true cannot be found. It is everpresent. Only our awareness of it comes and goes.

You cannot find your true Self because the part of you that looks for it is the very aspect that obscures it. Indeed, seeking truth is a nonsequitur. As soon as truth is sought, it becomes hidden.

The great conceit of western esoterica is that truth can be found. This is the inevitable result of a mind out of touch with nature and its own physical embodiment.

Truth is. It can be experienced in the moment, but it cannot be conceptualized. The mind cannot make truth. It can only receive it.

Truth exists before mindstates are created. That is why those who merge with truth are said to be of no-mind. No mind and truth are different names for the same thing. No mind is an empty reed. Thoughts come and go on the screen of consciousness; the breath enters one end of the reed and leaves through the other.

The reed is not dependent on the breath. Consciousness is not dependent on thoughts.

When thoughts die, consciousness remains. When the breath ends, the reed still holds the potential of sound.

It does not matter if the reed is ever picked up. It does not matter if another thought arises on the screen of consciousness.

When thoughts arise, there is awareness of thoughts. When thoughts no longer arise, there is just awareness.

That which is prior to thought exists in you. That which is prior to body or mind is your essence, but it cannot be found with mind or body. You cannot find the Creator through Its creation. Even if you investigate every aspect of creation, you will eventually come to the end of it. And at the end, there is the abyss. There, in that free fall, in that original explosion, you discover either that you are the Creator or that you are not. Either way, the game of seeking comes to an end.

Once you know who you are, you cannot give yourself away. You cannot lose yourself in some belief system, in some emotional state, or in some relationship. Who you are is not subject to where you go, who you are with, or what you do.

The true Self in you is not changeable. Everything may change around you, but that Self remains the same. No matter how your body looks or feels, no matter how many thoughts or emotions move through your consciousness, no matter if you are in a relationship or alone, that Self is the same.

Do you know that Self? Or do you know the one who changes with each thought, each emotion, each situation? Do you know the Creator or the creation?

This is not an abstract proposition. All suffering happens in the realm of creation. Emotional pain is felt when your life is experienced in reaction to the thoughts, feelings, and actions of others. You feel discomfort when you think that someone else is creating your experience.

When you know that you and you alone are creating your experience, albeit on many levels of consciousness, you stop playing the victim and blaming others for your problems. Instead of giving away your power to others, you claim full responsibility for what you think, feel and experience. You understand that you as creator give everything in your life the meaning that it has for you. You decide what is important and what can be overlooked. You decide where to put your energy, time and attention. If you invested your energy differently, your life would take a different course.

You know that no one else is responsible for the choices that you make. So you own all of your life, all of your choices, even those that you make at an unconscious level. The tapestry of your life is woven by these choices.

The thread itself is neutral. It has not committed itself to a particular pattern. It is willing to do the pattern you choose. The thread is consciousness. It is the empty vessel, awaiting your command, your interpretation, your investment. It is the open reed awaiting your breath.

You are one who decides what your life will be. You breathe life into every relationship and every circumstance which comes your way. Lest you gave it life, breath, meaning, purpose, it would have none. None of this exists outside of or apart from you.

Yet you think it does. The "you" you know is an effect, not a cause. This "you" identifies with outside things and defines itself in relationship to them. And so you are lifted up and dragged down, exalted and humiliated by all the myriad permutations of thought, emotion and experience. The "you" you know is affirmed by these identifications and injured by their perpetual rupture.

Why keep this drama going? Why seek stability and peace through the other? Why seek self-acceptance through the other's attention, approval, and validation? If you do, won't you be disappointed when the other's attention, approval and validation go away?

Why depend on the other for the love we must learn to give to ourselves? Why look for external approval, when we can find that existential affirmation of Self which is the ground of our being?

To be Self is to experience the most profound intimacy with all beings. There is no separation in the commitment to Self. It is the most generous and loving commitment one can make.

When each person is committed to truth within, honesty and clarity prevail in human relationships. Partnerships are based on inner strength and outer flexibility, not on emotional neediness and mental rigidity. Relationships between people who are committed to the true Self unfold in the present. They do not dwell on the past or live in anticipation of the future.

Those who are committed to Self know their relationship prospers the more they honor themselves and tell the truth to each other. Their dance with each other is no different than their dance with Self. It is the same dance.

As a result, they cannot give themselves away in the relationship. They can only celebrate the truth of who they are.

AUTHENTICITY

The authentic Self cannot be found in your narrowness, preconception, prejudice, or conceptual understanding, nor can it be found in the narrowness, preconception, or prejudice of others. Truth is beyond opinion.

The guru or teacher has no more of truth than you do. But, if the teacher is genuine, he or she may have less opinion, less prejudice, less narrowness, less need to argue, conceptualize, judge or condemn.

Having dissolved the barriers to truth for herself, the authentic teacher can help you recognize your own barriers. She cannot take you to truth, but she can show you how you stand in the way of realizing the truth that is already there in you.

The authentic teacher tells you that truth is within your heart of hearts. It is the essence of who you are, regardless of what you have thought, said, or done in the past. All that is immaterial.

However, to awaken to the truth that you are, you must be truthful. You must be honest with yourself and others. Until you tell the truth, you cannot be the truth.

Jesus said "I am the way." When you embrace the truth about yourself, you too will be the way.

The question is never "where is truth?" because truth is everpresent. The question is always "What is blocking the understanding of truth in this moment?"

As soon as you see what is blocking truth, you can surrender it. Then truth shines clearly through you.

Each person is a potential beacon of light, for the light is equally present in every being. But people are attracted to different trappings and conditions. Each trapping or condition is a lampshade dimming the pure

light of truth. Some lampshades are simple and unob-
trusive. They are hardly there at all. Others are
elaborate and very difficult to remove. They darken the
room. They make life seem darker than it really is.

Those who love you see the light within you. They
don't focus on the shadows you cast. They encourage
you to trade your elaborate lampshade in for a less
obtrusive one. They say "simplify your life" so that you
can see the light that is there in you and also in others.

Truth is not exclusive. It belongs to all equally.
Exclusive concepts of truth are delusional, no matter
what tradition they come from.

All of us will awaken when we are ready. For to
awaken is only to surrender all that is not true about us,
so that what is true can shine forth. All of us are bea-
cons of light hiding under lampshades of different
colors and size. And we always have the choice whether
we will see the light in one another or be preoccupied
with the lampshades.

God is not inside my narrowness or yours. But
when our hearts are open, God dwells within us.

Knowing this helps us to accept both our humanness and our divinity, our human imperfection and our divine perfection. It also helps us accept our absolute equality, for we are alike in our capacity for both delusion and clarity.

One Self

When I have realized my authentic Self, I desire your good equally with my own. I no longer believe that I can have anything of value by taking anything away from you. Indeed, I know that the more I give to you, the more I give to myself.

True Self is not what I see as "me." It is not what I see as "you." It is beyond all stratified concepts of "me" and "you." True Self is more accurately described as "me in you and you in me." It is the interpenetration of being. It is the consciousness that honors both of us in this moment.

When I see with my True Self I see only the True Self in you. To see with my True Self is to see beyond your mask, your appearance, to your essence. It is to see you through my love and acceptance of myself.

How I see you reflects how I see me. When I see myself with compassion, I can see you that way. Even if you call me terrible names, I will not respond in a fearful way, because I know from my own experience that these names describe how you feel about yourself. I know that you project your self-hatred on me because it is too scary for you to look at it. And I don't want to reinforce your self-hatred. So I respond to you in a way that recognizes your inherent dignity and your desire for acceptance.

When I can give you the love you would deny me, I give that love to both of us. I encourage you not to abandon yourself. I say "I have enough love for both of us. Since you cannot see love now, I will show it to you." And by doing so, I create a bridge over the separation you are feeling.

Every interaction I have with you offers me the choice to affirm who I really am or put on the mask of identity. When I put on my mask, I see you as separate from myself. I see your good and mine as different. And

I lose connection with what is most true about me and what is most true about you.

Most of us are convinced that the world we live in is a competitive one, a world of you vs. me, yours vs. mine, a world in which I am envious of your success, because I believe that what is good for you takes attention away from me. Is it any wonder that we experience struggle, sacrifice, selfishness, and greed?

But this competitive world is an illusion, a sad dream from which we can and will awaken. Our belief in this world keeps our masks in place and continues to recycle our fears.

This competitive world does not offer us true happiness or peace. Why then do we continue to believe in it? When will we be willing to see a different world?

True happiness is found when we let our masks fall away, when we accept the truth about ourselves and others, and stop competing with each other for love and approval. Then love belongs to all of us equally. And then it is not difficult to give or receive it.

PART FIVE

THE LESSONS OF

RELATIONSHIP

THE BETRAYAL OF SELF

It is very easy to betray yourself. All you have to do is say "yes" to others when you mean no. All you have to do is take someone else's identity for your own.

True intimacy is not possible for people who spend their lives trying to please others. One who seeks approval may find it for a while, but it is only a matter of time before that approval becomes a prison.

One who gives himself away will have to take himself back sooner or later. One who looks to another for salvation will blame that other when salvation does not come. One who says "yes" because she is afraid to say "no" will say "no" in the end, but it will not be a gentle, compassionate "no." It will be the harsh, unforgiving "no" of one trying to survive, of one afraid of suffocating. It will be the cry of one who feels betrayed, although in truth she has betrayed herself.

Those who have not individuated too easily borrow the identities of others. The roles they readily adopt to please you will be just as quickly abandoned when they don't receive the security from you they expect to find.

If you do not wish to be betrayed, do not let another person give herself away to you. Insist that she honor herself, for in honoring herself she will become capable of honoring you.

Co-creation happens between two equal beings. It cannot happen when one person is stronger than another.

When you love someone and he does not know what he wants, encourage him to find out. Hold the space for him to find out what he wants. He must learn this before he can come to you as an equal.

Don't be surprised when people come to you as a part with the expectation that you make them whole. It is a common occurrence. But don't take the bait. You cannot complete another, nor can another complete you. You must find your own completeness. You must know that you are already enough.

Don't think you will find another person who will

embrace you unconditionally before you have learned to do this yourself. It is not possible. At best, you can find someone to learn with.

PUSHING THROUGH

When a relationship ceases to be transformative for you, you will leave it. This is inevitable.

Of course, this isn't the only reason you leave a relationship. You also leave a relationship when you don't want to deal with the fears that are coming up for you.

However, rest assured, you will always create another relationship in which the same fears need to be dealt with. Just as you never stay in a relationship after it has served its purpose in your life, you cannot leave your relationship lesson before you learn it. You may need to experience that lesson with twenty different partners in twenty different ways, but you can't leave the lesson till you learn it.

Inevitably, you choose a partner who has a similar or complimentary lesson, and the same approximate degree of fear in learning it. Your partner will trigger your fear, and you will trigger his or hers, thereby bringing the lesson out into the open.

When that happens, you have a choice: project the fear onto your partner or own it. If you project your fear onto your partner, you make him or her responsible for everything that is wrong in the relationship and you never look at your own fear.

But if you have the courage to look at your fear honestly without making your partner responsible for it, you can push through to the other side. You can see all of the reasons why you avoid intimacy. And you can learn to love and nurture yourself, and begin to take genuine baby steps into intimacy.

When you are afraid, it makes far more sense to take baby steps then to leap into the fray. Of course, when you don't know that you are afraid, you will leap in, betray or be betrayed, and then wonder what went wrong.

As long as your fear is not consciously acknowledged, it will run your life unconsciously. It will create and destroy your relationships. This can be a somewhat painful way to learn.

You would find it easier to own your fear as it comes up. And thank your partner for helping you to become aware of it. Then your journey together can be a conscious one, one that embraces all of your fear, as well as all of your love.

SELF-NURTURING

The door to surrender in any relationship is guarded by the ego of each person. The ego wants the other person's support and acceptance, but it cannot give the same in return.

The ego is always trying to get its needs met by someone else because it does not know how to meet its own needs. It is always asking for something it doesn't have, or doesn't think it has. When two egos are in charge of a relationship, it never has a chance. It's either fight or flight, or both at the same time.

Surrender only happens when the ego steps aside. But it won't step aside until it feels acknowledged.

To acknowledge ego you must hear it. You must listen to its fears, its discomforts. You must let it know that you will not act in a way that increases its fears.

The process of listening to your fears is an ongoing one. As long as your buttons are being pushed in your relationship, you must listen and find out what your fear, your wanting, your neediness are all about.

After a while, you see without a doubt that there is no one on earth who could possibly address your fears. Not your partner. Not even you. All you can do is be present with those fears until an inner shift occurs.

Your awareness gradually brings that shift because your presence for yourself is an act of love. Seeing your fears and being with them creates profound psychological safety. It is the essence of the self-nurturing process.

In an intimate relationship, the first thing you try to do is to give this responsibility for self-nurturing to your partner. And your partner reciprocates by trying to give his or her responsibility to you. Once this happens and each accepts false responsibility for the other person's safety, the relationship will be driven by guilt and mutual projection.

Don't do this to yourself. Don't do this to your partner. Stand back and take responsibility for your own fears. Take the hand of your own wounded inner child. And let your partner do the same.

When your ego feels safe because you have been present with its fears, it will step aside. Only in this surrendered state can you meet the beloved.

All of your spiritual work is with your fears, not with your partner's. Being aware of your fears clears out a space for your partner to become present with you. This never fails.

The ego tries to love, but it cannot do it. It knows only how to want and demand. Love does not come from the ego. But it must come to the ego, from you. Your love for the fearful part of yourself creates safety.

When you bring love, ego is not a problem. It's only a problem when you are not bringing love. When you are not bringing love to yourself, the ego becomes fierce, almost insurmountable. The more you refuse to love and be responsible, the more awesome your ego defenses become.

Self-nurturing is the primary activity of spiritual life. When you are in a state of Self-love, you cannot find fault with yourself or others. You cannot feel insufficiency. So when you feel lack, you know it is time to bring love to yourself. When you are finding fault with your partner, you know it is time to bring love to yourself.

The search for love outside ourselves always ends in frustration and defeat. Our egos demand from others the nurturing and safety only we can give; and then we experience rejection and betrayal when others cannot meet our needs.

There are no good endings in this dramatic cycle. Every joining ends in a tragedy. Not because love is impossible or tragic by nature. But because the one who tries to love is the one in need of love.

Love Is Not Need

Demanding love in any specific form is an unloving act. Even if your lover were able to meet your demands, which rarely happens, you would still be unhappy. When one empty hole is filled from the outside, another one opens up. Wanting is a bottomless pit. No matter how much acceptance and approval you get from others, it won't be enough. That's because approval becomes addictive. The more you get, the more you need.

The approval of others is an unauthentic substitute for the self-acceptance you require. Only love of yourself satisfies, because it is self-fulfilling. It is not dependent on what anyone else says or does.

Suppose, for example, that you want to exercise on a daily basis. If you choose tennis, basketball or some other team sport, the integrity of your exercise schedule depends on the dependability of other people. If your tennis partner doesn't show up, you don't get the exercise you want.

If you choose yoga, running, walking or something you can do by yourself, you don't have to depend on others. Everything depends on your own commitment.

The same is true when it comes to acceptance and love. If you are committed to loving and accepting yourself on a daily basis, you feel loved even when other people aren't giving you praise or attention. You don't depend on others to feel good about yourself. You feel good about yourself and give others the space to feel however they feel about you.

It is not necessary that other people like you. It's nice when they do, but it should not be devastating when they don't. Self-worth must be established independently of the thoughts and feelings of other people. Then it is authentic. It is substantial. It is a reservoir of emotional strength that can be drawn on in times of emotional need.

Your need for someone else's attention has nothing to do with love. Love is the acceptance and nurturing you give to yourself, which naturally extends to others. When you take good care of yourself, your energy and enthusiasm are abundant and you are naturally supportive of others. You give them the space to be who they are. Because you are able to be who you are without apology, your presence is empowering to others.

People feel good in the presence of love. They do not feel good when presented with demands for love and attention.

Once you have learned to answer your own call for love, it is easier to deal with neediness in your partner. You see the hurt child in him and respond to him with compassion. You know that his need for love and your need for love are one and the same. No matter how awkwardly or inappropriately your partner asks for your love, you do not withhold love from him. You can do this because you have learned to love yourself through your neediness and your pain.

The more you answer the call for love in yourself and your partner, the easier it becomes to answer it wherever you hear it. You can see how the demands, the manipulations, the guilt trips others present to you are all camouflage hiding their naked cry for attention and approval. You hear that cry because it is your cry. It is the cry of all wounded children for love and acceptance.

Ultimately, the subject of love is not as complicated as we make it. As soon as we find one person we care about as much as we care about ourselves, we have found the door.

One person's unconditional love for another is what brings Christ forth in the world. When we answer the call for love, there are no needs left to be met. It matters not what we think is missing; when love arrives, it is missing no longer. Love is the universal solvent, the elixir of life, the question and the answer at once.

SEEKING IS NOT FINDING

For the love-seeker, even brief moments of happiness are tinged with grief. For the love-giver, every moment, happy or sad, is an opportunity to serve the beloved.

The love seeker and the love giver live in different worlds. You yourself live in different worlds depending on the role that you play.

If you are looking for love, making lists or demands on the other person, you are pushing love away. The harder you seek, the more you try to control, the more inaccessible you become to the presence of love.

The love seeker doesn't know how to love because she goes into her head and closes down her heart. She is concerned with what she is getting. She doesn't care to give any more.

Yet until she gives love, she will be miserable. Love cannot be withheld or imprisoned without destroying the lover. And when the lover is destroyed, all that remains is the small-minded needs of the ego.

Please recognize the disintegration that takes place here. In the beginning, you looked into your beloved's eyes with total acceptance. There was no fear of abandonment, no separation, no withholding of love. Now, you look into the same eyes through the lens of fear. Now you don't feel you are getting the love that you want.

This moment is inevitable in all relationships. Will you push through it gently and patiently, knowing it leads to the other side, or will you back off and choose not to enter the doorway? Will you go beyond selfish, conditional love, or will you insist on a love that meets your ego's needs?

If you listen to your ego, you will seek love perpetually and in vain. No matter how many partners you try, you won't find one who will love you the way you want to be loved. Because all your seeking is a demand for the love you alone can give.

But if you take a deep breath and push through these awkward moments when it doesn't feel like your partner is meeting your needs, you call yourself back to the heart. And there you learn to see the sparkle in your beloved's eyes that hides beneath her pain. She did not show you her pain at first, but surely you knew it was there.

It is there in you. It is there in your friends. Why

are you so surprised to find it in your beloved?

Look and see through the pain to who your beloved really is and what s/he really wants. That is the true beloved, the one who can lead you home. Not the one who pretends to have no pain. Not the one who promises to love you perfectly. S/he is just a sham.

Look to the real woman, the real man. The one who is vulnerable, who hurts, who asks for love in convoluted, neurotic, controlling ways. Look to him or her and hear the call for love behind the wound. That is the voice that will bring you home.

THE DIVINE DANCE

When you learn to accept yourself and your partner unconditionally, co-creation becomes possible. Then, in helping your partner, there is no betrayal of self. Instead, there is an expansion of Self consciousness that includes your partner's needs and interests. Then, the desire to please him or her other is no longer at the expense of yourself.

A relationship of this kind is a new psychological

entity. It is no longer "I" and "You." It is "Us." And this "Us" is greater than the sum of its parts, yet at the same time dependent on the ongoing functional integrity of the parts. If either person were to begin to betray self, the unity consciousness of "Us" would disintegrate.

Moreover, "Us" has its own life mission, made possible by the joining together of two individuated persons. That mission cannot be accomplished by either person acting separately. It can be accomplished only by the two listening together. The commitment of the couple to each other creates the environment in which their shared gift can be nurtured and given to the world.

This gift is rarely understood or brought to maturity. That is because most couples marry before they know who they are as individuals. They have not yet looked at their childhood wounds or come to conscious ownership of the fears and defense mechanisms that push away love. They have not explored their feelings of despair, inadequacy, and powerlessness. They have not found their faith or their purpose in life.

While it is possible to do this inner exploration

within the context of a life-long partnership, it is rare. Having projected their parental issues on their partners, most couples choose to separate from each other in order to individuate. It is a moot point that such separation from parental authority should have happened for both people prior to marriage. For most people it simply doesn't.

When individuation doesn't happen in a person's twenties or thirties, it often happens at mid-age. After a divorce, people learn to face their shadow side and own it. They learn to tell the truth to themselves and others. Thus, they bring greater honesty and integrity to their new relationships.

As difficult as a divorce may be, it does represent a second rite of passage, a kind of psychological rebirth in which the individual learns to embrace herself again, more deeply than ever before. No longer needing to please others at all costs, she affirms the truth about herself and lets go of what is false. She enters a process of ascension in which she learns to bring her true self to the altar of relationship.

PART SIX

KNOWING & NOT KNOWING

Not Knowing

What we know limits our experience. It prevents us from being open to what we do not know yet.

If our self-esteem is tied to what we know, we will feel personally threatened whenever our perceptions and worldview are challenged. Since we do not know all there is to know about anything, our lives are constantly presenting us with evidence that can broaden or deepen our knowledge.

If we have an "open mind," we are willing to learn as we go along. We understand that what we don't know is far greater than what we do know at any moment in time. We also appreciate the fact that much of what we take for truth today may be overturned by new evidence and experience tomorrow.

An open mind is a humble one. No matter how firmly convicted we are in our beliefs, we are willing to concede that there is another way of looking at things. By seeing that there are many possible interpretations of what happens, we can hold our own interpretation with flexibility and a sense of humor. We know that ours is not the only way to understand or perceive a situation. Indeed, our perception and our experience – while appropriate for us – may not be appropriate for others.

Having an open mind means that we are generous and compassionate with others. We respect their perceptions and experience, even if they are very different from our own. We understand that we can love and respect others and still disagree with the way they perceive the world.

To have humility is to understand the limits of what we know, to understand that there is a point beyond which we do not know. The humble person sees what she knows as a handful of sand, and what she doesn't know as the remaining sand on a beach that stretches out for miles.

What we don't know is always larger than what we do know. This includes what we know about ourselves, what we know about others, and what we know about the world. To realize that we know very little about anything does not denigrate what we do know; it just helps us hold that knowledge in a more flexible and compassionate way. It helps us hold that knowledge not as a weapon which we use to beat others, but as an invitation to dialogue and mutual discovery.

Conceit and intellectual pride stand in the way of our awakening. They short circuit our learning process. When we are hung up on what we know, we forget that we don't know very much at all. We begin to take ourselves far too seriously. And that means that we have fewer friends, more struggle, and less peace of mind.

Our need to be right in itself is an admission of egocentricity and self-righteousness. One who needs to be right rarely is, and when he is, it is at great price to himself and others.

If we want to live in a more peaceful way, we must recognize our need to be right as a sign of intellectual immaturity and emotional weakness. It does not serve our need to grow or be nourished in our relationships with others.

The ability to say "I do not know" without feeling unworthy is a sign of spiritual maturity. When we say "I don't know," we release our attachment to what we do know. And when we release that attachment, what we do know is either quietly confirmed for us or gently corrected.

NOT DECIDING FOR OTHERS

Perhaps the most important "I don't know" we can utter is in response to someone else's request for feedback or advice. Of course, it's always flattering to have someone ask for our opinion about something. But if we offer our opinion without being clear that it is our experience and interpretation, and that it may not work for that person, then we have not acted in a responsible way. And if we don't act responsibly now, the responsibility will come back to us later.

When someone asks for my advice, the responsible thing to say is "this is what has worked for me, but I don't know if it will work for you. I can't even be sure that it will work for me the next time I try it."

When I say "I don't know" in this way it tells others "You are responsible for what you believe and what you decide. So please consider it well. Listen to me and listen to others. But, most importantly, listen to yourself. You are the one who will make the choice and live with it."

Many people try to get us to agree with them or confirm their way of thinking. Our agreement seems to give their decision a sense of legitimacy. But what they are doing is asking us to become an authority for them. If we become the authority, then whatever happens — good or bad — is our fault. If it's good, we are put on a pedestal. If it's bad, we are crucified.

People who ask us for confirmation of their decisions are having difficulty taking responsibility for their own choices. Conversely, when we have a pattern of being an authority figure for others, we often live vicariously through others and postpone the decisions we must make in our own life.

When one person is an authority for another, neither is responsible for his or her own life. Our willingness to be an authority for others and to let them be an authority for us is more common than you might think. If you want to know how this applies to you, ask yourself "How often do I make my own decisions and encourage others to do the same?"

When we say "I know," we are saying that we are an authority for ourselves, if not for others too. When we say "I don't know," we are clear that we cannot be an authority for anyone else. Indeed, we recognize that we cannot be an authority even for ourselves, for what has been true for us in the past may not be true for us now.

Liberating ourselves from false responsibility for the thoughts, feelings, and actions of others is an important first step in the awakening process. Liberating ourselves from our own habitual thoughts, feelings and actions is an important next step.

DISMANTLING THE AUTHORITY OF THE EGO

What we believe and therefore energize in our lives comes from what we have experienced in the past. It is no wonder then that we continue to experience the same lessons over and over again until they make us thoroughly sick and disheartened.

If we want to have a different experience, we must have a different belief about ourselves. That is easily said, but not so easily done.

Before we can have a different belief about ourselves we must undo or neutralize the beliefs we already have. The best way to do this is to realize that they are just beliefs. They are not objective fact. Beliefs appear to be true, not because they necessarily are, but because we are invested in them.

Our emotional investment in these beliefs is the creative force in the manifestation process. As we believe, so do we act. These beliefs may be right or wrong, or a little of both. It doesn't matter. We create our life based on what we believe, regardless of how true or erroneous our beliefs are.

Reality unfolds in a way consistent with our beliefs so long as those beliefs are mentally clear and emotionally strong. When our beliefs are not clear and strong, things do not work in the way we think they should.

When there is an apparent conflict between what we want to happen and what happens in our lives, we can usually trace that conflict to our own inner ambivalence. Inner ambivalence is a sign that our beliefs no longer serve our growth and transformation. Something in our psyche no longer buys our old pictures and solutions. New solutions and pictures may not have come yet, but the old ones are being questioned, whether consciously or not.

Outer conflict and inner ambivalence go hand in hand. Both are a sign of transformation at work in the psyche. Old beliefs no longer hold our allegiance. And so our external life, which was built on the firm conviction of those beliefs, begins to fall apart as those beliefs shift from within.

An earthquake has begun in the psyche. The ground trembles and the edifices we have built upon it begin to sway. Glasses fall off the shelves. Furniture is upended. In some cases, even the most fundamental of our beliefs may begin to crack.

This external crisis is simply a reflection of our crisis of belief. We no longer believe as we used to. What we were sure about in the past is no longer a sure thing. What was black and white is now unfolding in various shades of grey.

Insecurity within. Revolution without. Each feeding the other until we lose track of which came first.

Mistakenly, we think the outer is the cause of the inner. This is a convenient fallacy that delays our having to take responsibility for what's happening in our lives. In fact, every major quake in our external lives can be traced back to a few tremors of uncertainty in the psyche.

Most of what we build in our lives will be reduced to ashes and dust. That is inevitable. What the mind creates must eventually be destroyed to make room for its new creations. All forms age and become obsolete. All buildings, no matter how painstakingly maintained, eventually decay and fall apart. There comes a point where the basic structure becomes untenable and cannot be repaired.

Beliefs too are gradually undermined from within. In time, they become weak, porous, overly stressed and stretched. Some develop gaping holes which are obvious to others but a mystery to us.

When our house falls down around us, we are the most surprised. What's obvious to our friends is often completely beyond our understanding.

That shouldn't be so surprising. When you are spending all your time and energy trying to shore up your house, it's hard to believe all of your efforts are in vain. Indeed, if you believed that, you would stop trying to fix things and just let them fall apart. You might even grab a sledge hammer and begin to help in the dismantling process.

Few of us are willing to grab the sledge hammer and dismantle our cherished beliefs, even when it has become obvious that they are not working anymore. We become attached to our own creations. And so the process of destruction happens unconsciously. Like an earthquake, it wells up from the depths of the psyche.

It seems to come from some inscrutable outside force, yet it happens with our soul's blessing. The soul gets tired of upholding beliefs which no longer serve its growth. So it reaches for the sledge hammer, while the conscious mind is screaming "watch out for the earthquake!"

Change always happens with our deepest blessing. No matter how much we moan and groan about our fate, we can be sure our soul gave its permission. For the soul is concerned with growth. And growth always means abandoning a restrictive form for one that has more room inside. All beliefs are expanded in this way until they cease to be limited.

So our conscious beliefs go from narrow to broad. As they broaden, they empower unconsciously-held complexes and defense mechanisms to surface into conscious awareness. This unconscious material is often at odds with our conscious experience, thus creating an inner ambivalence and tension that often undermines our plans and goals. Now, as these unconscious factors are brought into conscious awareness, the basis of our inner conflict can be acknowledged and released.

As conscious attention increases, unconsciousness decreases. That, in a nutshell, is what the awakening process is all about.

When our beliefs are very broad, when our minds are truly open, we accept most of the vagaries of human experience with caring and compassion. This caring and compassion is the mark of self-realized spiritual beings like Jesus and Buddha.

Each one of us is going through the same process of waking up or expanding our limited beliefs. When we learn to let go of what is no longer working in our lives, we make room for new awareness and experiences. As Jesus said, you don't want to put new wine into old skins. You need new skins for the new wine, new beliefs to contain and express the new awarenesses.

It all comes down to a simple question. Do we try to hold onto the past when it no longer serves our growth, or do we let it go and surrender to the possibility of a new experience? If we hold on, we will repeat our past experience in an exaggerated manner so that the pattern crystallizes and can be consciously surrendered. If we let go of our past experience, we begin to experiment with trusting a whole new belief about ourselves.

That new belief about ourselves is the beginning of our liberation from limitation and suffering in our lives. If we can prepare a space within where that new belief can be nurtured and sustained, the true self we are can be born within us and in our world.

To that end, we cannot look for reinforcement from without. Those who have supported us in our limited beliefs will not understand or be sympathetic to our birthing process. If we look outside of us for confirmation, all we will see is what is no longer working in our lives, all the roles that feel strange and uncomfortable to us now. The truth is, there is no place out there where we can fit in and be supported. We are the mother now. We are one providing the safe womb for the fetus. We cannot look without for support. Instead we must look within, find our strength within, believe in ourselves and the one who is being birthed through us. It is lonely going. But it is the only way the old is relinquished and the new is born.

OBSERVING THE OBSERVER

In our culture, knowledge is valuable. But knowledge is almost always about something or someone else. It is invested in the object of inquiry. It rarely turns its lens on the observer. Einstein, being a playful man, discovered that the observer was the one variable not being looked at. When he began to look at the one who was looking, a new world was revealed.

And so the West discovered something the East had known for some time: "it's not just what you see, but how you see it," or "what you see depends on how you see it."

In other words, there is no reality apart from the mind of the observer. All the objects in the world are experienced subjectively, by consciousness. Without consciousness there is no experience. When consciousness leaves the body, the awareness of the world leaves too. If, at that time, consciousness is not aware of itself, death is experienced as an ending of awareness, since there is no longer anything outside self to know.

If we want to understand the workings of the world, we will continue to study the object and how it behaves. If we want to understand the nature of consciousness, we will study the observer and how he sees.

When we study the observer, we notice that the life he creates for himself depends on the thoughts and emotions he holds in consciousness, whether consciously or unconsciously. Thoughts and emotions held in consciousness manifest outwardly as the events and circumstances of one's life. This does not necessarily happen in a linear way. In the same way that dreams are multileveled and multilayered, so are the events and circumstances of daily life, which are like a waking dream composed of thoughts and feelings woven together as leaves and branches are woven together by the wind. The patterns appear haphazard, but they are anything but that. They are amazingly precise. The wind always has its way quite specifically. If you knew its force and its direction and the resistance of objects in its way, you could predict the changes in the landscape.

But we will never know all this, no matter how sophisticated our scientific instruments become. The wind, we know all too well, is unpredictable by nature. It seems to be coming from one direction at a certain rate of speed and then its direction and speed shift. Gusts of wind, we call them.

There are gusts of wind in the heart and mind of the observer, perpetual changes of direction, impossible to measure or predict. The nature of reality is not random, but it is unpredictable. Only if you knew every factor in advance could you predict what would happen. But what are the chances that you or anyone anytime might know every factor in advance? Maybe not nil, but not far from it!

So are we to build our paradigm based on knowing, understanding that we will never realize it, or shall we build it on not knowing, understanding that is our ongoing existential stance?

To even consider building our paradigm on not knowing is a blow to the ego and the powers of the intellect. It immediately establishes humility, individually and collectively. It brings us out of our heads and into our hearts. It takes the focus off outer reality and shifts it inside. Now we are mindful of what we think and how we feel, because we understand that they are the content of consciousness, and we know that consciousness is creative. It will eventually outpicture, although we don't know quite how or when.

Now when things happen outwardly that we don't understand, we don't feel unfairly treated. We don't mope, pout, feel sorry for ourselves, nor do we blame others for what has happened. Instead, we look within.

We pay attention to our thoughts and feelings, without trying to change them or fix them in any way. We start tuning in, getting in touch with ourselves at a deeper level. And as we do, the process of manifestation slows down. We get to know the observer and we see how the observer is influencing the flow of reality. We see the conflict within our own consciousness, the conflict between what we think and how we feel, the conflict between what we want and what we need, the conflict between our conscious goals and our unconscious desires. And we stay with all that in a healing way. We accept it. We deepen. We let the polarities inform each other. And resolution of some sort begins to happen. Integration occurs in our act of being with our conflict.

Our "not knowing" brings us into the mysteries of Self and enables us to profoundly honor our subjective experience. However broken and incomplete our experience feels, there is a healing space where the pieces are accepted one by one and gradually fall into place.

When the observer is whole, everything he sees is holy. Heaven is not in the future, but here now.

You cannot reach this state from the outside in. You cannot reach it through striving. You reach it only by accepting and forgiving everything that happens. You reach it only by deepening inside, by pulling the outside in and owning it all. When that ownership is complete, there is no more separation between you and anyone else. That is where all the enlightened beings are. In that place where you are and have always been, not knowing it. Only now you know that you didn't know it.

Part Seven

Tao/Grace

Accepting Life As It Is

You do not ask for pain, yet it comes to you. And love comes to you in the same way: in a moment of total surprise. You may try to keep it, but it never cooperates. Like pain, love is sudden and elusive. Coming or going, it does not respond to the manipulations of your mind.

Consider this. If you are powerless to attract love or to make pain go away, what can you do except surrender? And surrender means simply that you accept what life brings to you in each moment. You accept it, because there is nothing you can do about it.

If you try to do something about your boredom or your pain, you will make them worse. Because this "doing" is from your ego, your dissatisfaction with life, your "try to fix it" attitude.

After many tries to "do" something about your emotional states, you eventually realize the utter futility of the proposition. There is nothing more to be done. Or to put it another way, enough has been done already. You have sufficient challenge to dwell with the doing you have already done.

In the beginning we think "more" is the answer to the perception of not having enough. More money, more activity, more lovemaking. But, in time, we learn that "less" works better. Less stimulation, fewer relationships, less external change – all lead to the deepening of experience. And in the deepening of experience, acceptance of the moment predominates.

Resting in the Heart

When you are in acceptance of your experience, you know how it feels. When you know how it feels, thinking and feeling run together.

Once you can feel your own pain, you have the motivation you need to end the conflict within yourself. But, you may ask, "don't I have this motivation from the beginning?"

Unfortunately, the answer is "no." If you knew the pain that would ensue when you ate the apple, you would not have eaten it. You had to eat the apple to know the pain.

That does not mean that the apple is bad. It doesn't even mean that pain is bad. In a sense, both are necessary to the experience of knowing. And all real knowing is a form of being.

That is why incarnation is necessary. You cannot know in a detached way. To know, you must become. You must experience. Knowing comes from being itself.

Many people attempt to find their spirituality through the "thinking" mind, but it never works. Thought can take you to the doorstep, but it cannot take you through the door. If you wish to enter the sanctuary, you must leave your concepts behind.

As you move deeper and deeper into the silence of the heart, the intellectual questions just fall away. It doesn't matter any more that the answers haven't been found. The answers become irrelevant as soon as the questions are dropped.

Once you have taken your first bite into the apple, you cannot give it back. You might as well finish it. That way you will complete the lesson and learn what you came here to learn.

THE MANIFESTATION PROCESS

People often wonder why a certain circumstance or condition manifests in their life. It may be because they have consciously asked for this condition, but this is rare. While prayer, affirmations and other efforts to concentrate the mind sometimes yield results, they do so only when there is a strong desire behind the mental practice. Wanting something mentally is not enough. We must want it with our whole being.

That which you desire you bring forth. What you want most, you promote without hesitation, drawing resources to you, enlisting the support and enthusiasm of others.

All manifestation is based on desire. Without desire, there is minimal manifestation. When you try to bring forth what you only halfheartedly want, you succeed only halfheartedly. But what you energetically and one-pointedly seek, overcoming all obstacles, comes to pass.

What you desire and think about all the time are seeds that you sow. And what you sow, you reap. Where you put your energy is where your life goes. Or, as the Master said, "Where your heart is, there will your treasure also be."

All it takes is your commitment. If you are ambivalent, uncertain, timid in your beliefs, they will not manifest clearly or strongly.

What manifests can be helpful or challenging. Usually, it is a mixture of both. Most manifestation comes from ego desire and, as such, it brings lessons and struggle, which help us to better understand and surrender the false self.

Sometimes we have the sense that we are building castles in the sand. We make elaborate structures, working in incredible detail, investing considerable time, energy and attention. And then the tide of life rises and takes what we have made away.

The creations of the ego are transitory by nature.

They are not meant to last forever. They are tools for learning that come and go.

Sooner or later, one comes to the end of ego creation. One gets tired of the drama one is creating. And then life slows down and simplifies. And there is no need to do anything in particular. Indeed, there is the awareness that anything I "need" to do will come back to haunt me. What I need is just more perceived lack that I look to fill from the outside...Another useless journey.

The manifestation process, as we know it, is ego-centric and fear based. We create out of the perception of lack. And because the perception of lack is so intense and steady, we are always making more and more stuff to try to fill the hole within.

The belief "I am unworthy" is the single source of environmental disaster on the planet. Because we feel unworthy, we are compelled to make and do a lot of "stuff" to prove to ourselves and others that we really deserve to be loved. If we could learn to bring love directly to ourselves, we would not have to project our unworthiness outward upon each other and the planet.

When we begin to take direct responsibility for loving and accepting ourselves in each moment, our outward activity is substantially curbed. The way others respond to us is only grist for the mill of our self-acceptance process. Gradually, we move from a manifestation process characterized by constant outward activity to a being process characterized by greater self-nurturing and less egoic search for happiness outside ourselves.

In our "being" process, it does not matter what happens so much as whether we are experiencing our own love and acceptance regardless of the outward form of our experience. Increasingly, happiness is understood and experienced as an internal event, not an external one.

When the desire for acceptance is no longer projected outward, the unhappy drama begins to dissolve. Unnecessary egoic activity comes to an end.

We no longer need to "do" or "make" to be worthy of love. We know that just by "being" we are worthy of love. And our inner worthiness enables us to give love without demands or expectations, thereby creating the pathway through which love spontaneously returns to us.

Our relationship to the world, and therefore to each other, is no longer one of manipulation, struggle or greed, but one of trust in the natural unfoldment of all organic processes, or in what the Chinese call Tao.

What needs to occur happens through us, because we are willing and able, not because our egos need it to happen to validate self. Tao unfolds in us and in all beings. When we respect this unfolding process, we are naturally drawn toward events and circumstances to which we can contribute our energy and attention.

This is spiritual manifestation, or the presence of grace. It is not based on personal desire, but acts for the fulfillment of all beings. It cannot seek one person's good at the expense of another's.

Spiritual manifestation happens without effort or attachment. Self worth is not on the line and so there is no need for a specific outcome. The expectations that arise are surrendered as one moves to embrace whatever is happening in the moment.

Tao creates spontaneously and impersonally. It has no favorites. Whatever it brings must be accepted. And in the acceptance of it, its inner meaning is revealed.

WILLINGNESS VS. WILLFULNESS

Grace is not something we can manipulate into being. It will not come when we try to coerce it into existence, even if we use gentle techniques like prayer and affirmation. Grace happens not through our willfulness, but through our willingness.

When we try to make something happen – it doesn't matter what it is – we perceive ourselves as needy or lacking and feel that we can't be happy without getting what we want. This attitude insures our unhappiness. Whenever we make our happiness conditional on something else or look for it in the future, we are disappointed.

By contrast, when we can be happy now without

demanding a certain outcome in the future, we do not establish the conditions for disappointment. When what we would like to happen does not occur, we know we can find our happiness in "what is." We are happy to keep doing this, because it is our spiritual practice.

Our energy is primarily invested in working in the present with what exists in our lives. We do this by releasing our attachment – positive or negative – to what happened in the past and being open to what might happen in the future. Being open means we may have some ideas about how we might like the future to be, but we are willing to be with it however it unfolds. We realize that we do not always know what is best for us, so when we ask for what we want, we remember to qualify our request with the words "if it is for the highest good of all concerned." This act of humility says: "I trust the universe to act appropriately."

When something happens that I don't think is appropriate, I can be unhappy or I can question my perceptions and learn to see things differently. I can feel disappointed, rejected, punished. Or I can accept the challenge to learn and to grow.

I find my greatest peace when I know that every-thing that happens in my life is perfect, even if I can't see how at the time. That is why acceptance must con-tinue to be my moment-to-moment spiritual practice.

Much of the magical thinking decked out in spiri-tual clothing is neither spiritual nor empowering. It forever places the cart before the horse. It says "I can be happy if...such and such happens." The emphasis is always on "such and such," not on being happy now. When I can be happy now, "such and such" is irrelevant.

All genuine spiritual practice is about being pre-sent and fulfilled in each moment. It doesn't matter if it is Christian, Buddhist, Jewish, Hindu, or Muslim practice. Present happiness, present acceptance, pre-sent love, peace and gentleness are the fruits of our spiritual practice.

Yet the dictum of the ego and the world is "I'll be happy now if I can have ____." You fill in the blank. In the face of this dictum, the voice of Spirit asks "Why not be happy now and trust Reality to unfold as only It knows how?" When we hear the voice of Spirit, we learn to put the horse first so that it can pull the cart.

When we are happy, we are immediately enlisted in the divine plan, which seeks only our happiness and that of others. We are given joyful and appropriate work in an instant. Imagine if someone came to you and said "Here are my skills. Please use them however you want to address our mutual good. I absolutely trust you to remunerate me in a fair and respectful way." You'd hire that person in an instant, would you not?

When you are willing to contribute without being attached to the outcome, you become a footsoldier for God. You cease to serve your own limited perception of what is good for you and begin to serve "the good of all."

That doesn't mean that you stop serving yourself. But you no longer serve yourself first. You serve first the one who is in most need of your help. And in serving that one, your own needs are met more profoundly than ever before.

Yes, the Kingdom of Heaven has its rewards. But if the rewards are separately sought, they dissolve before our eyes. Selfish motives must be transformed if we are to open to the law of grace in our lives.

When you give no thought to yourself, you give without conditions. You give with trust and faith. And so your gift has wings to find the one who cries out for it.

To give in this way is not sacrifice. If it feels like sacrifice, then you are giving with "too much thought" of yourself. What is given with self-consciousness or regret has no wings. It benefits no one. But what is given in good faith as it is requested in the moment serves others well and returns to the giver many times over. One who gives in this way lacks nothing of value and does not accumulate possessions that he does not need.

The Empty Vessel

When you know that you are loveable, and you no longer need anything in particular to happen in your life, you create an open space that can be filled with grace. Life calls to you and you follow, not because you have to, but because you are willing. You follow because life asks from you what you can easily and joyfully give. It does not demand sacrifice. It does not ask you to be responsible for what anyone else does. It neither asks you to lead, nor to follow. It simply offers you the opportunity to participate.

The flow of grace in your life is the beginning of the paradigm shift. You are no longer acting alone or in competition with others. Action is happening through you and through others in a collaborative way. It is a dance that you are part of. Your contribution is essential, but you are not the star of the show.

All of the stars are retired when the old paradigm fades into oblivion. In the new paradigm reality, everyone plays an equally important role. People are valued for who they are, as well as for what they do. Hierarchies are replaced by Equalities.

In the new paradigm reality, individuals are encouraged to listen to and follow their own guidance and to take responsibility for communicating their experience to others. When people aren't sure what they want to do, they are encouraged to take the time to find out what feels good to them. And they are asked to respect the need of others to get in touch with their own inner truth and make their own decisions.

New paradigm institutions do not seek to coerce or control the thoughts, feelings or behavior of their members. Members come together in appreciation of their individual uniqueness to address mutually formulated needs and goals. When those needs and goals are no longer shared, individuals are free to leave.

New paradigm institutions run not by the law of force, but by the law of grace. They come into existence to serve their members and they flow out of existence when the needs of their members are no longer served.

New paradigm institutions are democratic in the purest sense. Each person represents only himself.

Decisions in new paradigm organizations are made by group listening. Just as the individual has an inner authority that needs to be heard and respected, so does the group have its authority. This authority is recognized and its guidance spoken by any member who happens to be tuned into it at the time. When one member speaks the truth, other members feel it and align with it. In this way, decisions are made through intuitive consensus.

When the group is not in touch with its guidance and consensus is not available, no actions are taken by the group. Instead, time is taken to deeply hear what each person has to say, without any attempt to come to agreement. When everyone in the group can be heard without the pressure to decide, the conditions for receiving the group guidance are established. New paradigm groups understand that nothing of value can be hurried or forced. Patience is the rule of all decision making processes.

When decisions are made by intuitive consensus, the group can make choices that serve the greatest good of all its members. Attempts to arrive at such a decision through a rational, left- brain process usually fail, especially when there is a need to find agreement at the ego level.

As individuals align with the law of grace within their consciousness and experience, relationships will take on a new meaning. What two or more individuals could not do alone will happen spontaneously as they join together. The purpose of such relationships transcends individual needs and agendas, touching lives that never would have been touched otherwise.

Part Eight

Commandments
&
Uncommandments

HEARING OUR INNER VOICE

On the *Road to Nowhere*, there are no tablets of the law materializing on a sacred mountaintop, no burning bush, no special relationship with God. To be sure, there is a voice that is heard, but it is a small voice spoken in the heart, and everyone hears it in his or her own way. Hearing that voice is the beginning of revelation for each person.

Until the voice is heard, nothing in the world makes sense. Until the voice is heard, there is the conscious belief that one is in control of one's life, and the unconscious terror that one is a pawn in someone else's game. There is that duality in consciousness, that swing back and forth between false security and stark terror.

While there are no tablets of the law to guide us on the *Road to Nowhere*, there is a simple process that will help us stay focused in the present moment and hear the voice of truth within our hearts. I call this The Peace

Process, because it helps us move to that place of acceptance within which is large enough to contain all our contradictions and unfinished business.

THE PEACE PROCESS

#1 Trust yourself and listen within

You can have two types of relationships with yourself, a hostile one or a friendly one, one in which you doubt and disrespect how you think and feel, or one in which you listen to your thoughts and feelings with caring and compassion. Choose to trust yourself, and to listen patiently and kindly to all of the voices in your psyche.

#2 When you listen, don't think you
have "to know" or "to do" anything

You can listen within and hear all the different voices in your psyche without having to know the answer or to decide on a course of action. In fact, trying to find the answer or make the decision will put pressure on you, which will force you to disrespect one or more of the conflicting voices within you. When you do that, you are "forcing" a solution. Forced solutions never work. They only deepen the conflict. So don't force, just "be with" your situation. Feel it out. Get to know all of it. See both sides of the issue. Find your attachment to each end of the spectrum. Discover the pressure you put on yourself to know and decide. Investigate the landscape of your heart.

#3 As you investigate your thoughts

and feelings, keep your own counsel

No matter how tempting it is, resist the urge to get feedback from anyone else. Don't call your best friend, your therapist, your ex-husband or your mother. Even if your thoughts and feelings are about someone else, do not try to discuss what you are thinking or feeling with that person. Unless other people are familiar with this process of self-communion and support it, they will take you away from it. Instead, be fully with your own experience. Watch how it changes. Don't try to be consistent. Experience the inconsistencies, the swings from one pole to another. Fully be with all your conflict and ambivalence until you can appreciate all of it without needing to act on it or decide about it.

#4 When you can accept and be at peace

with all your thoughts and feelings, listen

to any intuitive promptings that arise

Wisdom flows from the state of peace and acceptance. By remaining in this state, you prepare yourself to receive consciously the wisdom that lies deep within you. That wisdom is there are all times, but it can be accessed only when you are in a state of inner trust.

As you open to all of the contents of your consciousness and patiently accept them, ask inwardly to be guided toward a solution that honors you and others equally. Pray for the highest good of all concerned and join with the divine will in wishing only good for all beings.

If you receive specific guidance while in this state, and you continue to feel peaceful as you consider the guidance you have received, begin to act on that guidance as soon as the opportunity to do so presents itself. Speak the words you are guided to say to others. Take the actions you are inwardly directed to take, even if you don't fully understand why you are taking them. Intuitive knowledge is based on "feeling right" about what you say and do, and not on coming up with an analytical solution. Later, as your look back on what happens, you may see why you were guided to speak or act in a particular way. Rarely, however, do you understand the whys and wherefores of your guidance before you act on it.

Often, the guidance you receive is not what you expect. That is because the guidance comes from a place of inner peace and psychic integration, in which all aspects of consciousness are patiently accepted. Solutions that come from this level of psychic integration often seem odd or peculiar to the ego mind that is looking at the problem or dilemma.

If specific guidance does not come when you try this process, do not be concerned. Often, when your inner conflict is acknowledged and accepted, any external difficulties just dissolve without your needing to say or do anything.

#5 As you follow your guidance, speak and

act toward others in a loving, respectful way

Realize that it is not what you do or what you say that is important as much as it is how you act and how you talk to people. Don't address others when you are not feeling peaceful. Wait until you can speak and act in a loving way. When you can speak the truth in a loving way, others can hear it without feeling attacked.

#6 However imperfect your words and

actions are, just accept them and know

that you have done the best you can

No matter how perfect your intentions are, you will never act or speak in a perfect way. Forgive your imperfections and reaffirm your desire for an outcome which honors all people.

#7 Accept the reaction of others, even

if they react in a different way than you

wanted or expected

What is important is that you took the opportunity to speak and act in a truthful and loving manner. How these words and actions are received depends on the choices made by the other person. You cannot be, nor should you try to be responsible for how others choose to react to you. Resisting their response will not improve it. Just remind yourself that others are doing the best they can and it is only their fear that prevents them from understanding your loving intention.

#8 If you are upset by how others react to you,

find a quiet place and begin this process again

The Peace Process is an ongoing one. It is to be undertaken whenever you feel confused or in conflict. Whenever the outer situation in your life is difficult for you to accept, this process gives you a way of being with your thoughts and feelings compassionately. It helps you come to peace within your heart and mind. You may have to do this process many times in relation to a particularly challenging person or issue in your life. That is okay. But please take your time and do each step fully, even if that step takes a few days to complete.

The Peace Process is not outcome-oriented. A specific outcome that is peaceful to you might not be peaceful for someone else. So please don't compare your guidance to anyone else's, even if the situations involved seem to be similar. Your consciousness is unique and, when you honor it fully, it will lead you to a solution that is uniquely peaceful for you.

COMMANDMENTS

Commandments are supposed to work for all people at all times, regardless of their situation. They offer us a ready-made, external answer to our suffering.

The people of Israel believed that the Ten Commandments represented their covenant with God. They believed that, as long as they obeyed God's commandments, they would be kept safe and free from suffering.

Unfortunately, as Job and others found out, fulfilling the law does not necessarily protect people from suffering. It is no different today than it was in Job's time. Good people get cancer and die. They get divorced, lose their fortunes, and see their children suffer. Keeping the commandments does not keep us or our loved ones safe. And conversely breaking the commandments does not insure punishment.

If there are rewards for keeping the commandments, those rewards are not often worldly ones. And, without worldly rewards, few people have the motivation to obey any set of laws, no matter how inspired they are.

When Jesus came on the scene, he saw that people were following the laws in a rote, lackluster manner. Their energy and attention was not in their actions. Their thoughts and actions were spiritually bankrupt and therefore could not raise their consciousness. Unless their consciousness could be raised, their awareness of the abundance and the good will of God would not be felt or understood.

So Jesus saw that his task was not just to teach the word of God but to inspire people to live from their hearts. He asked people not just to follow the letter of the law, but to get in touch with the spirit of the law as well. He asked them not just to refrain from killing or stealing or adultery, but to love their neighbors as they love themselves and even to love their enemies.

Jesus challenged the old teaching based on punishment. He told people their "eye for an eye" system of justice was not in harmony with the spirit of God's law. "If someone strikes you, turn the other cheek," he told his followers.

Jesus and other spiritually realized beings embody the teachings. They don't just read and recite the laws from a book or a scroll. They hear the voice of God within. They are in direct communion with the Source of the Commandments. So they know how the teaching is to be applied in each moment.

A system of external laws can never provide the specific guidance we need to live our lives in alignment with Spirit. In order to live in alignment, each one of us must learn to hear the voice of truth within our own hearts.

The law is not static. While it may come from the "absolute," the supreme Source, it must be expressed in a relative, conditioned world. Rigid applications of the law are neither insightful nor compassionate. They are punitive and without compassion for the individual and his or her unique circumstances. And so Jesus asked "who will throw the first stone?"

A teaching about love that is administered in an unloving way lacks integrity and must be challenged. When a spiritual teacher judges or attacks another person, he or she undermines the teaching. People see that the fruit of the teaching is rotten, and they reject the teaching. And well they should. Wise and compassionate spiritual teachers know that it is not just the words and concepts that are important, but also the way in which those words and concepts are expressed to self and others.

So Jesus tells us "by their fruits, you shall know them." He makes it clear to us that actions speak louder than words. If we want to understand a person's intention, we have to see how he or she acts. If we listen to the person's words only, we can be easily fooled.

Many people say all the right words, but they have no understanding. They are just repeating what others say. They are reading from a book. They are not in communion with their own experience, which is the only place genuine wisdom can be found.

That is why Jesus and other great teachers ask us not just to study what the tablets and commentaries say, but to be present in our lives in such a way that we are always listening for the direction of Spirit. They ask us to cultivate a direct relationship with God.

They are talking about process, not outcome. They are inviting us into a process of inner listening in which the truth can be heard and acted on. They do not tell us what that truth is in advance, because they want us to discover it in the moment.

THE GOLDEN RULE

When Jesus came on the scene, the Jewish people had 613 commandments covering almost every eventuality. Ordinary people could not understand the teaching. Even the rabbinical scholars disagreed amongst themselves about which behavior was appropriate under which circumstance. Is it any wonder that

Jesus said: "Let's keep it simple. Ten Commandments are enough; maybe even too much. Why don't we just focus on two?" By keeping the rules simple, more people can understand and obey them.

So Jesus streamlines the teaching so that we can begin to practice it, because he knows that only by practicing it will we start to understand it deeply. "Just remember this," he tells us: "Love God with all your heart and mind and love your neighbor as yourself." That will be sufficient.

Both of these injunctions are positive, present moment-oriented spiritual practices. To accomplish either of these practices requires all of our energy and attention.

To love God, we must realize that God is not only outside us, but within us. S/He is in our heart and our mind. S/He is intimate with us. Indeed, God's love and presence are the very essence of what we are. To love God means to love and honor ourselves, and to listen to and act on our guidance.

Yet just as God is our essence, S/He is also the

essence of each one of our brothers and sisters. And each of our neighbors deserves the self-same honor, love and respect that we do. To love God also means to love and honor our brother and sister, and to respect their guidance and the actions that flow from it.

We cannot love God and dishonor ourselves or our neighbor. Loving God is intimately connected with our love for ourselves and our love for other people.

When we fully grasp the meaning of these two simple commandments, we know what to do in all situations that present themselves to us. We need merely ask "How can I honor myself and my neighbor equally in this situation?"

This is the Golden Rule. It is easy to understand. It is hard to remember and to practice. Whenever we stray from the spiritual path, it is because we have forgotten this simple guideline which can transform the quality of our life.

All sin can be understood as the refusal to honor God within ourselves or God within our brother or sister. And as we mature in our practice, we begin to realize that when we forget to honor the other, we do not honor ourselves. And when we forget to honor ourselves, we do not honor the other.

In the end, we see that there is no "I" apart from "you" and no "you" apart from "me." And that is what Jesus wants us to understand. When we know this in the core of our being, we not only have full awareness of the teaching, we become the teaching. We model it in all that we do and say.

If we accept Jesus as our teacher, we must begin to keep the two commandments he gave us. We must begin to practice. We must see our whole life as a process of coming to peace with ourselves and peace with our neighbor.

And we must do so knowing full well that we will make mistakes. Just by staying with the practice he has given us, we will learn to forgive our own mistakes and the mistakes of others. For the practice is very deep and far reaching. There is nothing not contained in it. If we practice conscientiously, every aspect of our consciousness will be touched and transformed.

THE POWER OF HUMILITY

The ultimate issue is always about what we know and do not know. When we think that we know a lot, we don't leave much room for learning and growth.

When we are proficient in our study of the laws — be it the laws of the Talmud or Koran or the laws of mathematics or physics — we think we know what can or should be done. We are content with the explanations that are given to us. It doesn't take long before that passive acceptance of what we have been taught becomes intellectual conceit. Then, we think our knowledge is the only truth.

Openmindedness is an essential aspect of humility. To be humble, we must recognize the limits of what we know. Indeed, we must recognize the limits of most forms of knowledge, which are based on what we have experienced in the past. While our previous experience may be authentic, it may not serve us in this moment.

Genuine knowledge is intuitive and present-oriented. It is what helps us right here and right now.

When we "know" in this way, we don't just know in our heads. We also know in our hearts. Knowing like this has wholeness and clarity. There is no argument or deliberation.

All attempts to analyze or figure things out come from not knowing. Deliberation is not knowing pretending to know. It leads us deeper and deeper into conflict. Only when we realize that we don't know does not knowing become an asset. New awarenesses then become possible.

Pretending to know when we don't know is the primary architect of personal illusion. Genuine ignorance is never a problem. When you don't know, you can learn. You are teachable. But when you don't know and think that you do know, you are not teachable. You have established a block to learning.

Letting go of those blocks is what the spiritual path is all about. It is not about learning so much as it is about removing the blocks to learning. Learning when we want to learn is never very hard. A motivated learner learns without great effort.

So the major lesson for all of us is to stop pretending to know what we do not know. That pretense keeps our ignorance in place. And ours is not the ignorance of innocence, but the ignorance of experience, as Blake would have it. It is the conscious refusal to give up pretense and admit that we don't have the slightest idea of what we are talking about.

When we admit that we do not know and indicate our desire to learn, teachers spontaneously appear to help us. Life gloriously hears our call and provides us with the most intricate and beautiful opportunities to expand our consciousness. The prayers of the one who cries out in honesty and humility are responded to fully. The universe mobilizes to our simple cry for help.

But the one who pretends to know is a stranger to such assistance. Thinking he knows, he does not attract those who can help him in his ignorance. And so he closes his heart and continues his pretense until he is in so much pain that he drops his facade and cries out for assistance.

Those who knock on the door will find that it is

opened to them. Those who stand at the door too proud to knock will not be heard, but that is their own choice.

God does not withhold love or truth from anyone. But only those who have open hearts and minds will experience it. Our job is not to discover love or find the truth, but merely to remove the barriers that keep both from us. When our hearts and minds are open, all the gifts of God can be entrusted to us.

PART NINE

BEING WHERE WE ARE

Romance And Despair

The romantic view of life and the despairing view of life are both interpretations. The romantic view says that life is full of wonder and meaning, and that love and beauty are to be sought and savored. The pessimistic view says that life is difficult, without noble purpose, and that love and beauty exist, if at all, just for a few fleeting moments. For any experience we have, there is a romantic interpretation and a pessimistic or despairing one.

If we look beneath either interpretation, we will find reality as it is. It is neither beautiful nor ugly, noble nor ignoble, loving nor unloving, or perhaps it is both extremes at the same time. Things are simply as they are. When we can let them be, without interpretation, the beauty we touch is informed by sadness, the love we know is deepened by grief, and our passion is heightened by feelings of separation.

To experience life in its wholeness is rare. More often than not we experience one side of the equation.

We experience our affection for our spouse or lover at one time, and our disaffection at another time. When our ego is pleased, we feel happy and elated. When our ego is wounded, we feel sad or angry.

When we are sad, we do not think of all the happy moments in our relationship. And when we are happy, we don't think of all the difficult times. So we swing back and forth from happy to sad, from pleased ego to wounded ego.

This pendulum-like movement back and forth between the extremes of our mental and emotional experience is typical for most of us. It happens no matter whom we are in relationship with. When we have the opportunity to spend long periods of time in seclusion, we can appreciate the veracity of this statement. The ups and downs of our emotional experience do not originate with any other person. They originate in our own consciousness.

In this sense, it doesn't matter whom we are in relationship with. We will continue to experience the same ups and downs that we do when we are alone. In most cases, however, these extremes will feel even more intense with a partner than they do when we are alone. Our pleasure and our pain will be heightened because our partner shares it with us. Now, when we are happy, we can look into the eyes of our beloved and see incredible joy and celebration. But the opposite is equally true. When we are angry or sad, we can look into the eyes of the other person and see merciless disconnection and judgment.

We mistakenly think that the other person is making us happy or sad, but this is not true. This is the illusion of the drama we are engaged in. We want to make other people responsible for what we are thinking and feeling. For some reason, it is very hard for us to admit and take responsibility for our negative thoughts and feelings. Yet, until we can do this, we cannot get off the wheel of trespass or karma.

To admit that we judge, dislike, hurt and attack other people helps us get in touch with the depth of our own self-judgment and self-hatred. By acknowledging our negative thoughts and feelings, we no

longer give them the power to run our lives unconsciously. When our buttons are pushed and we begin to
react to another person, we remember that the other
person is just triggering own storehouse of negativity.
And we stop making the other person responsible for
our unhappiness.

That is what it means to hold another person innocent. We can look at that person and see his pain and
misery, a perfect reflection of our own, yet we know
that he is not the cause of our pain, nor are we the
cause of his.

Relationships give us the opportunity to withdraw
our projections and own them. Everything we think
and feel about our partner belongs to us, not to the
partner. The partner just gives us the chance to look at
our own stuff. This may be hard to remember when
that person is attacking us, but that is why relationship
is a demanding spiritual path. Whenever any conflict is
experienced in a sacred relationship, both people must
be willing to own their unhappiness and let the other
person off the hook.

Arguing with the other person, trying to convince him that you are right, or trying to fix him are absolutely futile. They are just more projection on your part. Your peace does not lie in fueling the conflict or continuing the projection. Your peace lies in stepping back and saying to yourself "I see that I am upset and unhappy and that I think that my partner is the cause of how I feel. But I know that this can't be. I know that I alone am responsible for everything that I think or feel. I am responsible for how I see my partner and how I see my partner is my interpretation, my judgment of who that person is. It is not who he is, even if his behavior seems to match my perceptions of him...I and I alone am responsible for how I think and feel right now."

If you can do this process internally when you are in conflict with another person, you can literally stop that conflict instantaneously. One way to facilitate this is for both people to agree to take time out from the conflict and spend time alone taking responsibility for the thoughts and feelings that are coming up in consciousness. Then, if necessary, the conversation can be continued after both people have owned their judgments. When both people take full responsibility for how they feel without blaming the other person, the basis of conflict is dismantled and each person can look at the other again with openness and love.

MIRROR, MIRROR ON THE WALL

There is a difference between being a cause of something and being a reflection of it. Your partner's anger can be a reflection of your own anger without being a cause of it.

Say, for example, you are angry, but you are not conscious of your anger. So when your partner gets angry at you, you respond back in anger. You feel justified in your anger, because you are just responding to your partner's attack on you. You weren't angry at your partner until she attacked you, or so you maintain.

But the truth is you were angry; you just weren't aware of your anger. Your partner's anger triggered your anger and feelings of separation. It brought them up for you to look at. If you can look at your own anger and feelings of separation, instead of focusing on what your partner is feeling or doing, you can make a breakthrough here. You can stop being a victim and understand that your anger belongs to you and you alone. It wasn't caused by someone else. The most anyone else could do was to trigger an expression of what you were already feeling.

Your angry response to your partner is the key. It tells us your anger was there to begin with. If, on the other hand, you responded to your partner's anger with compassion, that would tell us there was no anger in you to be provoked.

When we respond to someone else's attack compassionately – when we turn the other cheek as Jesus would have us do – we stop the vicious cycle of projection, mutual trespass and karma. We let the other person know that we refuse to participate in the game of shame and blame. Instead, we say to the attacker "I am innocent and so are you."

We recall that person to the truth about herself.

We do not complain about her behavior or make her wrong for it, nor do we respond to her attack with defensive behavior or an attack of our own. We show her who we really are – not the person she thinks she sees – and we invite her to be who she really is, free of the guilt she carries and tries to lay at everyone else's feet.

To stand for who we really are in the face of someone else's attack is not to be a wimp. It takes great courage and great compassion. Jesus does not ask us to be a doormat, but to be who we are in all our strength and splendor.

When we don't accept the attack, we don't give anyone reason to feel guilty, nor do we take on any guilt ourselves, because we have not responded in an attacking way.

Most of us feel that it is extremely difficult to "turn the other cheek, love our enemies," or respond to attacking behavior in a compassionate way. That is the case because we do not understand our connection to the attack. We don't understand that it is our feelings of separation that need to be looked at. They are what take our peace away. And so, ultimately, they are what we must address. In this sense, the other person's provocation is a gift to us. It helps us get in touch with feelings of separation we are not acknowledging.

If we blame the other person or make him responsible for our anger, we will miss the opportunity to grow into greater self-responsibility and peacefulness. Our peace will depend on whether or not the other person expresses sorrow for his actions and does not repeat them. We cannot afford to make our happiness and peace dependent on someone else's choice. That would not be fair to us or to the other person.

Our happiness and peace are and can only be our responsibility. If we are angry, we must stop focusing on the external "cause" or trigger of our anger, and see it instead as a reflection of an anger that was already there in us, although unknown and unseen. That which brings up our buried anger and judgment is our best teacher, hard as this may be to accept. But we don't have to love the teacher to accept the lesson. Love and respect will come in their own time when the lesson has been learned.

Much of our suffering arises from our attempt to make the reflection into a cause. While everything in the outside world reflects our ever-changing state of consciousness, nothing out there is the cause of how we think or feel. The responsibility for how we think or feel belongs only to us.

Our greatest spiritual challenge is to be responsible for our own thoughts, feelings and actions and to encourage others to take similar responsibility for their own lives. We are not here to judge others, to make decisions for them, or to try to change their ideas or their feelings. Nor are we here to invite others to judge us, make decisions for us or try to change our ideas and feelings.

If we will accept responsibility for our own con-sciousness and experience, and offer other people our acceptance and respect, we can undo the cycle of pro-jection. Then we can live in the state of inner peace and outer freedom that Jesus and other Christ-realized beings attained. That state, they promised us, is here for us to claim whenever we are ready.

Facing The Music

As long as we put our attention outside our own consciousness, thinking that other people are the cause of our happiness or our pain, we will be locked in an unnecessary interpersonal power struggle. The outcome of this struggle is inevitable. We cannot win, nor can the other person. Both of us are losers.

The outer search will always come up empty. It never delivers what it promises.

Sooner or later we have to face the music. There isn't anyone or anything out there who is going to love us, save us, take care of us, give us what we want when we want it. Our ego's version of paradise does not exist.

This is a difficult fact for most romantics to face. Yet, based on their track record, you wonder why. Haven't you noticed that most romantics have tragic relationships? Indeed, you can make the argument that romantics experience more tragedies than do pessimists, because romantics have higher expectations.

If you want great "Romeo and Juliet" type tragedy, put two romantics together. Neither will live up to the other's expectations. And they will keep pushing each other's buttons until they are totally beaten to an emotional pulp. Romantics "never say die," but they rarely stay together for more than six months.

Obviously, having high expectations of other people isn't the answer to our relationship quandaries. But neither is the pessimist solution of doing our own thing and having no expectations of the partner at all. While romantics are bouncing in and out of relationships with great melodrama, pessimists are growing gargantuan roots in relationships that lack energy and intimacy.

Do we have to choose between a relationship that has wings but no stability and a relationship that has roots but no wings? That seems to be the choice that most people make. Yet either choice is limiting.

The romantic needs a dose of realism. He needs

staying power, patience, a better sense of boundaries. The pessimist needs less rigid boundaries and more hope, trust, and willingness to explore and take risks.

Every relationship has both polarities. The challenge for each partner and for the relationship as a whole is to grow both roots and wings. Each person needs nurturing and stability, as well as challenge and growth. And if both people are integrating these polarities within their own lives, there is a better chance that they will be able to find this balance in their relationship.

It would be foolish to suggest that this kind of integration is easily accomplished either for the individual or for the relationship. In both cases, it tends to be a lifetime work requiring great commitment, emotional resilience, patience and humor.

AWARENESS OF SEPARATION

Oftentimes, we think we know what we need in our relationship, but we're wrong. What our ego thinks it needs has nothing to do with what we really need. In that sense, we don't know what we need, because we can't see the big picture.

Our relationship is not a known quantity, but a mystery. It is not static, but is constantly changing and unfolding. If we are wise, we stay in the present and learn to move with it. We stay away from analyzing it, or trying to make it fit our pictures of the way we think it should be.

To be fully present in our relationship, we must accept it as it is in the moment. If we are not accepting it here and now, we will increase the separation we feel from our partner. Comparing our relationship as it is to some ego-ideal of what a relationship should be is not accepting the relationship as it is.

When we move out of the "is" space into the "should be space," separation is inevitable. This happens so quickly it requires a great deal of alertness to even see it. Usually, we don't notice it until the separation builds and anger or hurt trigger our awareness of it.

But separation is happening all the time. It is happening every time we want to change our partner or want to make our relationship different from the way it is.

These separation thoughts would be happening for us even if our partner were not in the picture. They would happen with another partner or with no partner. The nature of our ego is to find fault with our experience, to compare it to some unattainable ideal. Our ego says what happens isn't good enough. Our relationship is not good enough. Our partner is not good enough. That is its perpetual litany.

When this litany of lies is running, you either become aware of it or you don't. When you become aware of it, you see the untruth and stop participating in it. When you are not aware of it, you "accept" these thoughts unconsciously or semi-consciously. You allow the lies to dominate your consciousness.

When Jesus encountered an untruth, he responded "get thee hence Satan." He never allowed a lie to go unchallenged. For forty days he did this in the desert. If we were willing to do it for forty days, some of us might wake up too.

Lies must be challenged where they are: in consciousness. It is not enough just to challenge the lies that are spoken. We must challenge the unspoken lies as well, the thoughts we entertain in consciousness, knowing full well that they are not true.

Our spiritual practice calls us to challenge every unloving thought we have about ourselves or other people. As long as these thoughts go unchallenged, we will feel separate from our true Self and the true Self of others.

The challenging of falsehood does not stop when we enter a relationship with another person. Indeed, it intensifies. Now, we must challenge not only our unloving thoughts about ourselves, but our unloving thoughts about our partner. That is why relationship is such a profound path to the divine.

SURRENDERING OUR CONCEPTS OF PERFECTION

Our ego's idea of perfection is always at odds with our experience. But genuine perfection is never at odds with what happens in our lives. However, to see that perfection, we usually have to surrender our ego-expectations and our prejudicial interpretations of what happens.

Often the act of surrendering involves understanding that what we think means "something" really means "nothing," or at least doesn't mean what we think it does. We must negate or undo the meanings we want to impose on reality.

"Nothing" is the antidote to "something." When we need to do something, it is because we feel that something is wrong or something is lacking. But when there is nothing that needs to be done, we recognize the perfection of what is and abide with it.

In the same manner, "nowhere"' is the antidote to "somewhere." When we need to go "somewhere," we believe that there is something wrong or inappropriate about where we are. When we know that there is nowhere to go, wherever we are is acceptable.

The ego is always lobbying for us to do something or go somewhere. It is convinced that there is some lack in us that we can fill by some kind of activity. As a result, many of us spend a great deal of our time and energy trying to change "what is" in favor of "what should be."

When we do this, we don't find satisfaction. New things and places eventually become old and we take them for granted. Then, the need to "change what is" rises again, and keeps rising, every time we indulge it.

The alternative is to accept what is unconditionally and look instead at why we want it to be different. When we become aware of our resistance instead of indulging it, it shifts. We stop pushing our life away and learn to open to it, even when it doesn't meet our expectations or match our pictures.

As a spiritual discipline, each of us would do well to spend some time each day doing nothing and going nowhere. When we can learn to be where we are, without needing to do anything in particular, we can find the meaning that is already there for us. That meaning/purpose doesn't come from us, although we are the ones who recognize it. Yet it is a treasure that awaits us at all times.

FORGIVENESS MEDITATION

Forgiveness practice is a major aspect of meditation, because every thought or action which involves a judgment needs to be forgiven. Since many of our thoughts and actions involve judgment, we have plenty of forgiveness work to do whenever we sit down to meditate.

To forgive is not to do, but to undo.

To undo a judgment, we say to ourselves "the judgment I made is untrue. It was made in ignorance. It says more about me than it does about anyone else. But it is not even true about me. This judgment is a reflection of my fear. I will be with my fear rather than judge another or myself."

To forgive your judgments in this way is to be with yourself in compassion. It is the training ground for being with others.

The same practice can be undertaken when you are upset about judgments others make about you. If Saul says something nasty about you to a mutual friend, say to yourself: "The judgment Saul made is untrue. It was made in ignorance. It says more about him than it does about me. But it is not even true about him. This judgment is a reflection of Saul's fear. He attacks me because he doesn't want to face his fear. I in turn want to defend myself because I don't want to face my fear. Saul and I have the same fear and neither he nor I wants to face it. I accept the fact that Saul's behavior brings up fear in me. And I am willing to be with my fear now, instead of trying to defend myself."

If you undertake this practice with respect to your judgmental thoughts and actions toward others and those of others toward you, you can undo these judgments in your psyche. When you are free of judgment, you are present and clear. You feel a deep peace and bliss. That is the fruit of meditation.

You can do forgiveness meditation anytime you want to. You don't need a formal time or place, although in the beginning you may find that a formal time and place is helpful.

When you do forgiveness meditation, you take responsibility for undoing judgment and attack in your consciousness. You claim the peace that is available to you and offer it to others as a reminder of what is also available to them.

Some of the greatest actions we can take are non-actions, moments in which we undo what we have done and unthink what we have thought. This is the essence of forgiveness practice. It has very little to do with forgiving others. It has everything to do with forgiving ourselves for our unhelpful thoughts and actions toward others, as well as for our defensive reactions to the unhelpful thoughts and actions of others toward us.

MOVING BEYOND EGO

It is inevitable that a book like this one would leave you with forgiveness practice. Even though you may accept the premise that it doesn't matter what you do or where you go on the *Road to Nowhere*, chances are you are in judgment of what you have done or where you have been. If you are in judgment of the past, you will try to fix it. And the more you try to fix it, the less acceptable and whole it will seem to you. The way to peace is never to create new agendas for perfection and new expeditions in search of redemption. Perfection and redemption either happen now or they never happen.

Either you are at peace with the past right now or you are at war with it. Either you are finding forgiveness now or you are finding fault with someone.

So let's put aside doing and accept the challenge of undoing what we don't feel good about. Let's undo our suffering at the root. Let us find the compassionate being in us who is beyond the smallness of our ego, yet not opposed to our ego's cry for love and acceptance.

Let us find the compassionate being who loves and accepts our ego, as well as the egos of others. For that which accepts egoic experience without judgment is beyond ego. It is aligned with love, with the non-dual essence of who we are.

All complicated psychological states can be reduced to two simple ones: the state of being aligned with love and the state of being in the grip of fear.

The state of fearfulness arises from the judgments we make about others and ourselves. It is that simple. When we stop making these judgments, the mechanism of fear is dismantled.

The apostle Paul was right. Love is the greatest of all human capacities. Yet we know very little about love. Most of our experience is about judgment.

If we need to teach people to love in order to find redemption, we may be here a very long time. Fortunately, we don't have to do this. Our salvation does not require us to learn how to love. Our salvation requires only one thing: that we stop judging ourselves and others. That is all. When we stop judging, we automatically connect to love. We don't need to know how to do it. It just happens.

And how do we stop judging except to become aware of our judgments and undo them at their source? We practice forgiveness right here, right now.

You can practice forgiveness on the *Road to Nowhere* just as well as you can practice it on any other road, perhaps more easily. Because when you are on the *Road to Nowhere*, you don't get mesmerized by the signs along the way that promise luxury hotels in exotic destinations. On the *Road to Nowhere*, you know you are just where you are right here and right now. When you are a committed traveler on the *Road to Nowhere*, you know that salvation isn't somewhere else at some other time. So you just keep looking at the contents of consciousness and forgiving all the judgments that come up.

On the *Road to Nowhere* you learn that every judgment you make is connected to some fear that is coming up for you. So you stop justifying the judgment and denying the fear. By acknowledging both, you allow them both to be undone.

When you realize that you are in fear, you can move out of it. It's only when you deny the fear that you get stuck in it. Emotional honesty is a very helpful skill on the *Road to Nowhere*.

When you feel separate from someone, it doesn't matter "why" you feel separate. "Why" is irrelevant.

Worse, it is a smoke screen. When you go off trying to find out "why," you lose sight of the fact that, regardless of "why," separation means that fear is coming up for you. And fear only comes up when you are making judgments of someone.

The trail to self-discovery does not lie in understanding why things happen, but in understanding "what" is happening here and now.

When I see that I am not at peace, when I acknowledge my isolation from my deep self, my brother, and God, I open up a space of awareness which immediately connects me to Self, other and God. When I see my own fear, I open to the place in me that fear covered over.

If I can't see my own fear, then I will see everything through it. But if I can see my fear, I can lay it aside. And then I will see what is really there.

When we remove what is false, we automatically come to the truth. It is instantaneous. We peel back the layers of disguise and discover the essence behind them. When we own our fear, love quietly announces itself.

Many of us are looking for God somewhere out there. But since God has never existed apart from us, our external pilgrimages are in vain. When we think God isn't who we are or who our brothers are, we find only persecutors and victims.

If we seek peace in form, we see that form is easily broken and tends toward chaos. Only if we seek peace in our own hearts can we find forgiveness for all the broken pieces of our experience. And then we can learn to bless the world with our acceptance and our love.

A FINAL BLESSING

Nowhere is not a bad place. It's just the place you come to when you stop avoiding this moment. It is just the place you come to when you realize that the journey doesn't have to do with anyone but you.

You are the subject: your thoughts, your feelings, your words, and your actions. If you are willing to turn your attention to these, then you will enter the path that Jesus, and Buddha, and all the enlightened ones walked. Christ or Buddha is not a particular person, but a state of awareness that can be attained by each one of us. We become the Christ or the Buddha when we make peace in our hearts and in our relationships, as Jeshua and Gautama did.

The Buddhists say that if you should meet Buddha coming along the road, you should kill him. That is because the Buddha is not some holy character who deserves special treatment. The Buddha is each one of us.

What Buddha can do, every one of us can do. And not just in the future or in some other place. We can do it right here, right now.

When enlightenment comes, our light shines everywhere on all things. Whatever path we enter is acceptable. Whoever we meet along the way is welcome. There is no reason to try to manipulate the journey to bring us to some magical destination, because no place on the *Road to Nowhere* is any more important than any other place.

When we come to the end of special places and special people, anywhere and anyone will do fine. That

213

is the universal heart and mind that is born in us through our forgiveness practice.

May you find that heart and that mind. They have always been there in you.

Namaste.

Paul Ferrini is the author of numerous books which help us heal the emotional body and embrace a spirituality grounded in the real challenges of daily life. Paul's work is heart-centered and experiential, empowering us to move through our fear and shame and share who we are authentically with others. Paul Ferrini is the editor of *Miracles Magazine*, a publication devoted to telling Miracle Stories that offer hope and inspiration to all of us. Paul's conferences, retreats and *Affinity Group Process* have helped thousands of people deepen their practice of forgiveness and open their hearts to the Divine presence in themselves and others. For more information on Paul's workshops and retreats or *The Affinity Group Process*, contact *The Miracles Community Network*, P.O. Box 181, South Deerfield, MA 01373 or call 413-665-0555.

New From Heartways Press and Paul Ferrini

• **Waking Up Together**
Illuminations on the Road to Nowhere

There comes a time for all of us when the outer destinations no longer satisfy and we finally understand that the love and happiness we seek cannot be found outside of us. It must be found in our own hearts, on the other side of our pain. "The Road to Nowhere is the path through your heart. It is not a journey of escape. It is a journey through your pain to end the pain of separation."

This book makes it clear that we can no longer rely on outer teachers or teachings to find our spiritual identity. Nor can we find who we are in relationships where boundaries are blurred and one person makes decisions for another. If we want to be authentic, we can't allow anyone else to be an authority for us, nor can we allow ourselves to be an authority for another person.

Authentic relationships happen between equal partners who take responsibility for their own consciousness and experience. When their buttons are pushed, they are willing to look at the obstacles they have erected to the experience of love and acceptance. As they understand and surrender the false ideas and emotional reactions that create separation, genuine intimacy becomes possible, and the sacred dimension of the relationship is born. 216 pp. paper ISBN 1-879159-17-1 $14.95

● **The Ecstatic Moment:**
A Practical Manual for Opening Your Heart and Staying in It.

A simple, power-packed guide that helps us take appropriate responsibility for our experience and establish healthy boundaries with others. Part II contains many helpful exercises and meditations that teach us to stay centered, clear and open in heart and mind. The Affinity Group Process and other group practices help us learn important listening and communication skills that can transform our troubled relationships. Once you have read this book, you will keep it in your briefcase or on your bedside table, referring to it often. You will not find a more practical, down to earth guide to contemporary spirituality. You will want to order copies for all your friends. 128 pp. paper ISBN 1-879159-18-X $10.95

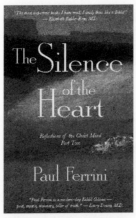

● **The Silence of the Heart**
Reflections of the Christ Mind,
Part Two

A Powerful sequel to *Love Without Conditions*. John Bradshaw says: "with deep insight and sparkling clarity, this book demonstrates that the roots of all abuse are to be found in our own self-betrayal. Paul Ferrini leads us skillfully and courageously beyond shame, blame, and attachment to our wounds into the depths of self-forgiveness...a must read for all people who are ready to take responsibility for their own healing." 218 pp. paper. ISBN 1-879159-16-3 $14.95

Heartways Press
"Integrating Spirituality into Daily Life"
More Books by Paul Ferrini

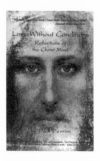

• **Love Without Conditions:
Reflections of the Christ Mind**
An incredible book from Jesus calling us to awaken to our Christhood. Rarely has any book conveyed the teachings of the master in such a simple but profound manner. This book will help you to bring your understanding from the head to the heart so that you can model the teachings of love and forgiveness in your daily life. 192 pp. paper ISBN 1-879159-15-15 $12.00

• **The Wisdom of the Self**
This ground-breaking book explores our authentic experience and our journey to wholeness. "Your life is your spiritual path. Don't be quick to abandon it for promises of bigger and better experiences. You are getting exactly the experiences you need to grow. If your growth seems too slow or uneventful for you, it is because you have not fully embraced the situations and relationships at hand...To know the Self is to allow everything, to embrace the totality of who we are, all that we think and feel, all of our fear, all of our love." 229 pp. paper ISBN 1-879159-14-7 $12.00

• **The Twelve Steps of Forgiveness**
A practical manual for healing ourselves and our relationships. This book gives us a step-by-step process for moving through our fears, projections, judgments, and guilt so that we can take responsibility for creating the life we want. With great gentleness, we learn to embrace our lessons and to find equality with others. A must read for all in recovery and others seeking spiritual wholeness. 128 pp. paper ISBN 1-879159-10-4 $10.00

• The Circle of Atonement
The Wounded Child's Journey
Into Love's Embrace

This book explores a healing process in which we confront our deep-seated guilt and fear, bringing love and forgiveness to the wounded child within. By surrendering our judgments of self and others, we overcome feelings of separation and dismantle co-dependent patterns that restrict our self-expression and ability to give and receive love. 225pp. paper ISBN 1-879159-06-6 $12.00

• The Bridge to Reality

A Heart-Centered Approach to *A Course in Miracles* and the Process of Inner Healing. Sharing his experiences of spiritual awakening, Paul emphasizes self-acceptance and forgiveness as cornerstones of spiritual practice. Presented with beautiful photos, this book conveys the essence of *The Course* as it is lived in daily life. 192 pp. paper ISBN 1-879159-03-1 $12.00

• From Ego to Self

108 illustrated affirmations designed to offer you a new way of viewing conflict situations so that you can overcome negative thinking and bring more energy, faith and optimism into your life. 128 pp. paper ISBN 1-879159-01-5 $10.00

• Virtues of The Way

A lyrical work of contemporary scripture reminiscent of the Tao Te Ching. Beautifully illustrated, this inspirational book will help you cultivate the spiritual values required to fulfill your creative purpose and live in harmony with others. 64 pp. paper ISBN 1-879159-02-3 $7.50

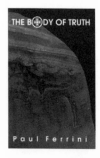

• The Body of Truth

A crystal clear introduction to the universal teachings of love and forgiveness. This book traces all forms of suffering to negative attitudes and false beliefs, which we have the ability to transform. 64 pp. paper ISBN 1-879159-02-3 $7.50

• Available Light

Inspirational, passionate poems dealing with the work of inner integration, love and relationships, death and re-birth, loss and abundance, life purpose and the reality of spiritual vision. 128 pp. paper ISBN 1-879159-05-8 $12.00

Guided Meditation Cassette Tapes
by Paul Ferrini

• The Circle of Healing

It's finally available. The meditation and healing tape that many of you have been requesting for months is now here. This gentle meditation opens the heart to love's presence and extends that love to all the beings in your experience. A powerful tape with inspirational piano accompaniment by Michael Gray. ISBN 1-879159-08-2 $10.00

• Healing the Wounded Child

A potent healing tape that accesses old feelings of pain, fragmentation, self-judgment and separation and brings them into the light of conscious awareness and acceptance. Side two includes a hauntingly beautiful "inner child" reading from *The Bridge to Reality* with piano accompaniment by Michael Gray. ISBN 1-879159-11-2 $10.00

• Forgiveness: Returning to the Original Blessing

A self healing tape that helps us accept and learn from the mistakes we have made in the past. By letting go of our judgments and ending our ego-based search for perfection, we can bring our darkness to the light, dissolving anger, guilt, and shame. Piano accompaniment by Michael Gray. ISBN 1-879159-12-0 $10.00

Heartways Press
Order Form

Name_____

Address_____

City _____State _____Zip _____

Phone _____

BOOKS

Waking Up Together ($14.95)   _____

The Ecstatic Moment ($10.95)   _____

The Silence of the Heart ($14.95)   _____

Love Without Conditions ($12.00)   _____

The Wisdom of the Self ($12.00)   _____

The Twelve Steps of Forgiveness ($10.00)   _____

The Circle of Atonement ($12.00)   _____

The Bridge to Reality ($12.00)   _____

From Ego to Self ($10.00)   _____

Virtues of the Way ($7.50)   _____

The Body of Truth ($7.50)   _____

Available Light ($10.00)   _____

TAPES

The Circle of Healing ($10.00)   _____

Healing the Wounded Child ($10.00)   _____

Forgiveness: Returning to the Original Blessing ($10.00)   _____

SHIPPING

($2.00 for first item, $1.00 each additional item.

Add additional $1.00 for first class postage.)   _____

MA residents please add 5% sales tax.   _____

                                   TOTAL $_____

Send Order To: Heartways Press
P. O. Box 181
South Deerfield, MA 01373
Tel: 413-665-0555

Please allow 1-2 weeks for delivery